Applying Evaluation Criteria Thoughtfully

OECD))

This work is published under the responsibility of the Secretary-General of the OECD. The opinions expressed and arguments employed herein do not necessarily reflect the official views of OECD member countries.

This document, as well as any data and map included herein, are without prejudice to the status of or sovereignty over any territory, to the delimitation of international frontiers and boundaries and to the name of any territory, city or area.

The statistical data for Israel are supplied by and under the responsibility of the relevant Israeli authorities. The use of such data by the OECD is without prejudice to the status of the Golan Heights, East Jerusalem and Israeli settlements in the West Bank under the terms of international law.

Note by Turkey
The information in this document with reference to "Cyprus" relates to the southern part of the Island. There is no single authority representing both Turkish and Greek Cypriot people on the Island. Turkey recognises the Turkish Republic of Northern Cyprus (TRNC). Until a lasting and equitable solution is found within the context of the United Nations, Turkey shall preserve its position concerning the "Cyprus issue".

Note by all the European Union Member States of the OECD and the European Union
The Republic of Cyprus is recognised by all members of the United Nations with the exception of Turkey. The information in this document relates to the area under the effective control of the Government of the Republic of Cyprus.

Please cite this publication as:
OECD (2021), *Applying Evaluation Criteria Thoughtfully*, OECD Publishing, Paris, *https://doi.org/10.1787/543e84ed-en*.

ISBN 978-92-64-48199-2 (print)
ISBN 978-92-64-98402-8 (pdf)

Foreword

Evaluation plays a critical role in informing the design and delivery of policies and programmes that lead to better – fairer, more sustainable – development outcomes. Evidence from evaluation, and the critical thinking evaluation can support, play a crucial role in helping decision makers and communities ensure policies and programmes deliver positive, lasting results for people and the planet.

To support evaluation practice, in 1991, the Organisation for Economic Co-operation and Development (OECD) Development Assistance Committee (DAC) published definitions of five evaluation criteria. These criteria have shaped the design and evolution of international development evaluations over the past 30 years. The criteria are widely recognised as playing a central role in improving the quality of global evaluation practice and supporting collaboration. They have enabled organisations to design and deliver evaluations that are relevant to the needs of decision makers and capture a wide range of intended and unintended results, producing valuable evidence and insights.

These five criteria were further adapted in 2018-19. The revision process drew on nearly three decades of learning by members of the DAC Network on Development Evaluation (EvalNet) along with the wider global evaluation community. It was informed by the 2030 Agenda for Sustainable Development, including the Sustainable Development Goals (SDGs), and the Paris Agreement within the United Nations Framework Convention on Climate Change (UNFCCC). A new set of definitions, including two principles guiding their use, was published in December 2019.

This guidance complements the criteria definitions and their principles for use. It aims to support thoughtful and contextualised application of the criteria. Through the inclusion of questions and examples the guidance encourages critical reflection and nuanced analysis. The guidance will assist readers as they consider how to interpret and apply the criteria to improve the quality of their evaluations and better support learning and accountability.

Learning about how best to use these adapted criteria – in international development co-operation and beyond – has only just begun. The intention is to continue to gather lessons and insights from their use and to revisit this guidance based on the collective experience and feedback from the global evaluation community. Particularly valuable will be lessons coming from new ways to use the criteria that better reflect the principles of the 2030 Agenda, such as evaluations that are participatory or apply a human rights based approach, evaluations of complex change processes, and evaluations that capture synergies and trade-offs in holistic ways.

Acknowledgements

The Secretariat would like to thank the global evaluation community for rich discussions and debate on the criteria over the course of 2017-19, which contributed to identifying the need for this guidance and helped shape its content. In particular, the National Evaluation Capacity (NEC) conference participants, the United Nations Evaluation Group (UNEG) and the Evaluation Co-operation Group (ECG) were key partners in the adaptation of the criteria and input from many of their members is reflected here. The Secretariat is grateful for contributions from evaluation partners around the world, and welcomes discussion to further develop this working draft guidance.

This document reflects extensive contributions from the members of the Network on Development Evaluation (EvalNet), a subsidiary body of the Organisation for Economic Co-operation and Development (OECD) Development Assistance Committee (DAC). EvalNet members contributed many useful comments and insights on the draft criteria definitions and engaged in detailed discussions on the concepts contained in this document. In many cases, this involved extensive discussions within member agencies and ministries, as well as consultation with development evaluation stakeholders. EvalNet members provided input on their own experiences and challenges with the criteria, including concrete examples, which helped to bring the document to life. EvalNet's Working Group on Gender Equality contributed to developing relevant elements of this guidance. The Secretariat also gratefully acknowledges the instrumental role of EvalNet Chair Per Øyvind Bastøe in shepherding the adaptation process and the development of this guidance.

Megan Grace Kennedy-Chouane led the development of this guidance for the OECD, with support and input from Rahul Malhotra, Hans Lundgren, Alison Pollard, Ola Kasneci, and Yee King Ho. Many other colleagues from the Development Co-operation Directorate provided feedback on earlier drafts. Andrew Brenner and Suzanne Parandian provided editorial feedback. Stephanie Coic and TFK provided graphic design on the images and figures.

Ima Bishop, Joe Watkins and Nick York (IOD PARC) drafted the guidance and provided invaluable input to its content. Julia Betts provided peer review and feedback, in addition to contributing extensively to the initial criteria revision process, the new definitions and their conceptualisation.

Table of contents

Tables

Figures

Boxes

Abbreviations and acronyms

3ie	International Initiative for Impact Evaluation
AfDB	African Development Bank
ALNAP	Active Learning Network for Accountability and Performance in Humanitarian Action
BMZ	German Federal Ministry for Economic Co-operation and Development
CEDAW	Convention on the Elimination of All Forms of Discrimination Against Women
CRPD	Convention on the Rights of Persons with Disabilities
DAC	Development Assistance Committee
Danida	Danish International Development Agency
DEval	German Institute for Development Evaluation
DFI	Development Finance Institution
DFID	UK Department for International Development
ECG	Evaluation Co-operation Group
EU	European Union
FAO	Food and Agricultural Organisation
GIZ	Deutsche Gesellschaft für Internationale Zusammenarbeit
ICAI	UK Independent Commission for Aid Impact
IEG	Independent Evaluation Group, World Bank
JICA	Japan International Co-operation Agency
NGO	Non-governmental organisation
Norad	Norwegian Agency for Development Cooperation
ODA	Official development assistance
OECD	Organisation for Economic Co-operation and Development
SDG	Sustainable Development Goal
Sida	Swedish International Development Cooperation Agency
SMART	Specific, Measurable, Attainable, Relevant and Timely
UN	United Nations

UNEG	United Nations Evaluation Group
UNFCCC	United Nations Framework Convention on Climate Change
UNHCR	United Nations High Commissioner for Refugees
WFP	World Food Programme

Executive summary

The Organisation for Economic Co-operation and Development (OECD) has established common definitions for six evaluation criteria – relevance, coherence, effectiveness, efficiency, impact and sustainability – to support consistent, high-quality evaluation. These criteria provide a normative framework used to determine the merit or worth of an intervention (policy, strategy, programme, project or activity). They serve as the basis upon which evaluative judgements are made.

The criteria can be thought of as a set of lenses, providing complementary perspectives that together give a holistic picture of an intervention and its results. The criteria encourage evaluators – as well as those involved in designing or managing interventions – to think more deeply about the nature of an intervention, its implementation process and its results.

Two guiding principles were set out by the OECD DAC Network on Development Evaluation alongside the definitions of the six criteria. These are:

1. Principle One: The criteria should be applied thoughtfully to support high-quality, useful evaluation.
2. Principle Two: Use of the criteria depends on the purpose of the evaluation.

The criteria should be applied thoughtfully and adapted to the context of the intervention and the evaluation. Though originally developed for use in international development co-operation, the criteria can be applied in any sector and for evaluations of public or private interventions. They can be used to evaluate many different topics and types of interventions – including thematic topics or strategic issues, policies and projects. Different methodologies can be used when evaluating based on the criteria, recognising that the criteria form just one part of the full spectrum of evaluation norms and standards.

Evaluators should work in ways that thoughtfully consider differential experiences, and reflect how power dynamics based on gender and other forms of discrimination (e.g. age, race/ethnicity, social status, ability) affect the intervention's implementation and results.

The key concepts for each of the criterion are defined as follows:

- Relevance entails examining the extent to which the intervention's objectives and design respond to beneficiaries' needs and priorities, as well as alignment with national, global and partner/institutional policies and priorities. Understanding gendered power dynamics and reflecting on the commitment to "leave no one behind" are crucial in understanding relevance. If circumstances change, evaluations should also look at whether interventions remain relevant.

- Coherence – the new criteria – examines the extent to which other interventions (particularly policies) support or undermine the intervention and vice versa. This includes internal coherence (within one institution or government) including compatibility with international norms and standards, and external coherence (with other actors' interventions in the same context). Coherence includes concepts of complementarity, harmonisation and co-ordination, and the extent to which the intervention is adding value while avoiding duplication of effort. In line with the 2030 Agenda, greater attention must be paid to coherence, with an increased focus on the synergies (or trade-offs) between policy areas. This new criterion encourages an integrated approach to understanding complex interventions and their results.

- Effectiveness looks at the extent to which the intervention achieved, or is expected to achieve, its objectives and its results, while taking into account the relative importance of the objectives. The new definition encourages analysis of differential results across groups and the extent to which the intervention contributes to or exacerbates equity gaps. Effectiveness is the most commonly evaluated criteria and is often used as an overall measure of success.

- Efficiency helps evaluators ask questions about the extent to which the intervention delivers, or is likely to deliver, results in an economic and timely way. "Economic" is the conversion of inputs (funds, expertise, natural resources, time, etc.) into results, in the most cost-effective way possible, as compared to feasible alternatives in the context. The new definition includes the dimension of "timely delivery". This criterion is an opportunity to check whether an intervention's resources can be justified by its results, which is of major practical and political importance. Many stakeholders, including beneficiaries, care about efficiency, because it can support better use of limited resources, to achieve more.

- Impact is the extent to which the intervention has generated or is expected to generate significant positive or negative, intended or unintended, higher-level effects. Impact addresses the intervention's ultimate significance and potentially transformative effects – holistic and enduring changes in systems or norms. The impact criterion goes beyond effectiveness and encourages consideration of the big "so what?" question. This is where evaluators look at whether or not the intervention created change that really matters to people.

- Sustainability is the extent to which the net benefits of the intervention continue or are likely to continue. Depending on the timing of the evaluation, this may involve analysing the actual flow of net benefits or estimating the likelihood of net benefits continuing over the medium and long term. While the underlying concept of continuing benefits remains unchanged, the new definition encompasses several elements for analysis – financial, economic, social and environmental – and attention should be paid to the interaction between them.

A variety of challenges may be faced when applying each of the criteria, including common issues related to weaknesses in intervention design and data availability. Practical suggestions are provided for how evaluators and evaluation managers can overcome these challenges, including by assessing evaluability early in the process, working with stakeholders to document decision made or recreate baselines, and being transparent about any limitations to manage expectations. These tables – and the rest of the guidance – will be updated as further lessons from experience are gathered.

1 Purpose and use of the guidance: Better criteria, better evaluation

This chapter explains the purpose of the document and how it can support readers in understanding the adapted criteria definitions and use them in their work. It also explains how the guidance was developed, including the role of global evaluation stakeholders in informing its design and content. The chapter then considers how the criteria should be applied thoughtfully to improve both the delivery and design of evaluations.

Why guidance is needed

The OECD's Development Assistance Committee (DAC) first laid out five evaluation criteria in 1991 (OECD, 1991[1]) and provided definitions for them in 2002 (OECD, 2002[2]). These five criteria – relevance, effectiveness, efficiency, impact and sustainability – have become a common reference point for evaluators in development co-operation and beyond.

Prompted by a desire to respond to the 2030 Agenda and the opportunity to draw on extensive experience and learning since the criteria were first defined, a wide-ranging consultation and adaptation process was undertaken in 2017-19 and revised criteria definitions were endorsed by the DAC in December 2019 (OECD, 2019[3])[1]. During the consultation process, users indicated that they found many aspects of the evaluation criteria to be valuable and would like to continue to use them in their assessment future interventions. The feedback showed that the evaluation criteria are widely used and understood, allowing for consistency and a certain level of comparability.[2] They have created a common, simple and neutral language as well as a normative framework in the sector that is adaptable, results-focused and comprehensively covers the key areas required for accountability and learning. As a result, the revised criteria reflect support for continuity and build on what worked well with the original definitions.

The guidance should be read in conjunction with the OECD's *Quality Standards for Development Evaluation* (OECD, 2010[4]) and the *Principles for Evaluation of Development Assistance* (OECD, 1991[1]). The *Principles* focus on the management and institutional setup of evaluation systems whilst the *Standards* inform evaluation processes and products. This guidance helps users to operationalise the definitions of the evaluation criteria by unpacking them in more detail, providing examples and discussing the practical challenges commonly encountered when they are implemented during evaluations. Box 1.1 notes future publications that will further support application and understanding of the criteria.

Over the last 25 years, much has been learned about how to use the criteria set out by the DAC. The main challenge identified during the 2017-19 consultation was their practical application. The discussions underlined the importance of how the criteria should be used and not just how they are defined. For example, the criteria are sometimes used in a mechanistic way and not tailored to context. The idea of the guidance is therefore to support different user groups in the thoughtful application of the criteria in practice, contributing to higher quality, useful evaluation.

Accordingly, the document includes language and guidance to help readers understand and apply the criteria definitions, including the two principles elaborated to guide the use of the criteria (OECD, 2019[3]). This guidance expands on these two principles and explains each criterion's definition, enabling users to interpret and apply the criteria in their work.

The purpose of the guidance and how to use it

This document provides users with a succinct guide on how to interpret the criteria and apply them thoughtfully in their work. While the criteria are primarily applied in evaluation, they have wide applicability in monitoring and results-based management, the design of an intervention, or in strategic planning. It is intended to help users think through some of the challenges that can arise and where to look for solutions. It helps readers understand how to unpack the definitions, how the criteria relate to each other, the challenges when applying them and how these challenges can be addressed. Practical examples have been selected to illustrate how the criteria can be thoughtfully applied in real-world settings.

The guidance is not intended to be used as an evaluation manual, template or checklist. This guide is one source to draw on when evaluation plans are being developed and may also help to complement institution-specific policies, standards and guidance on which evaluators rely.

Box 1.1. Further work and forthcoming OECD evaluation publications

In addition to revisiting this guidance based on experience with the new definitions, EvalNet and partners are also developing specific guidance that will go into more depth on particular topics, including guidance for use of the criteria with a gender equality lens as well as the application of the criteria in humanitarian settings. In collaboration with EvalNet, ALNAP is also in the process of updating its widely used guidance for humanitarian evaluation and use of the criteria (Beck, 2016[5]).

Translations of the criteria definitions and principles

Working with key partners, and in line with the mandate to support learning and evaluation capacity development, the OECD is currently in the process of translating the criteria definitions into various languages in addition to the official languages of the OECD, English and French. Translations into Spanish and Chinese have been completed with new versions in Arabic, Dari, Pashto, Portuguese, Russian, Thai, and Urdu expected in 2021.

2nd Edition of the Glossary of Key Terms in Evaluation and Results Based Management

Definitions of the five original criteria were first published in the OECD's *Glossary of Key Terms in Evaluation and Results Based Management* (OECD, 2002[2]). A second edition of the *Glossary* is currently being developed, reflecting updates to the criteria and other terms. The (forthcoming) *2nd Edition* will be a useful companion to this guidance, as it provides succinct definitions of words used throughout the text, including: results, outcomes, impacts, theory of change, and beneficiary.

Equally, the guidance does not replace existing ethical guidelines and standards, as set out by other institutions or proposed by the OECD DAC (OECD, 1991[1]; OECD, 2010[4]). The guidance complements international standards used by the United Nations and other multilateral agencies, such as, the United Nations Evaluation Group (UNEG) norms and standards, Evaluation Co-operation Group (ECG) good practice standards and Active Learning Network for Accountability and Performance in Humanitarian Action (ALNAP) guidance. Other useful resources include the websites of bilateral, UN agency and other multilateral evaluation units, the Better Evaluation website and the websites of EvalPartners and its related agencies, which focus on specific areas such as the International Initiative for Impact Evaluation (3ie).

By the same token, the guidance, like the criteria themselves, is intended to prompt self-reflection and critical thinking and is not to be used in a mechanistic way. Such an approach is out of sync with best practice and the principles of 2030 Agenda (described further in Chapter 3). The guidance does not prescribe specific methodological approaches or tools, as the criteria are not a methodology. Some signposts to other sources that do elaborate on methods are included in the document as a starting point.

The guidance can be seen as a bridge between the overarching, formal documents such as the definitions of the criteria (OECD, 2019[3]) and OECD Quality Standards (OECD, 2010[4]), which provide consistent and clear definitions and terminology, and the day-to-day application of the criteria in particular institutions in a thoughtful and appropriate way, with the many context-specific decisions that this requires.

In addition to providing examples of how the criteria have been applied in real evaluations, the guidance includes elements for analysis that explain the concepts contained within each definition. These elements are not intended to be definitive or used as discrete or sub-criteria, but rather they illustrate and help to unpack each definition. They will assist users in finding the best contextual interpretation of each criterion for an individual evaluation. During the design phase, dialogue between evaluators, commissioners, and intended users of the evaluation's findings can also explore how the different elements of each criterion should be assessed and which are most important in drawing overall conclusions, as this will vary depending on the intervention, context and intended use of an evaluation.

Chapter 2 introduces the role of evaluation criteria and how these fit within broader norms and standards. Chapter 3 provides guidance on how to interpret the criteria and apply them thoughtfully, and will also help evaluators in using the criteria within their policy context. In Chapter 4, each definition is described in more detail, common challenges are highlighted and practical examples given. Reflecting the 2030 Agenda policy priority to "leave no one behind", Chapter 4 includes an overview of key issues related to inclusion to consider for each criterion.

As most of the examples are drawn from evaluations based on the original definitions, and the new definitions and principles are only now being rolled out, this guidance is considered as a working draft. The guidance will be used during a testing phase of initial implementation and then be revised after several years to capture additional learning and up-to-date examples. The Secretariat is particularly interested in gathering more examples from beyond the EvalNet membership and lessons on the use of the criteria for local and national evaluations.

Who can use this guidance?

The guidance is applicable for use across a range of contexts – local, national and international. The criteria are deliberately broad and have been designed for applicability to a range of interventions and sectors. They are relevant beyond the traditional sovereign official development assistance interventions. If applied thoughtfully, the criteria can be equally useful to interventions related to the private sector, blended finance or similar policy areas such as trade, amongst others.

This guidance is intended primarily for evaluators, evaluation managers and commissioners. It is suitable for students or young professionals using the criteria for the first time, as well as seasoned practitioners carrying out complex evaluations. It will also be of interest to guide intervention design, strategic planning and results management. Better evaluation depends partly on an effective integration of monitoring, evaluation and learning systems within the programme or policy cycle. The guidance will be useful in helping evaluators and operational partners develop a shared vision of and language about what success looks like at the outset (i.e. during the design phase of an intervention), making interventions more assessable, while improving overall results.

References

Beck, T. (2016), *Evaluating Humanitarian Action using the OECD-DAC Criteria*, ALNAP, [5] https://www.alnap.org/help-library/evaluating-humanitarian-action-using-the-oecd-dac-criteria (accessed on 11 January 2021).

OECD (2019), *Better Criteria for Better Evaluation: Revised Evaluation Criteria Definitions and Principles for Use*, DAC Network on Development Evaluation, OECD Publishing, Paris, https://www.oecd.org/dac/evaluation/revised-evaluation-criteria-dec-2019.pdf (accessed on 11 January 2021). [3]

OECD (2010), *Quality Standards for Development Evaluation*, DAC Guidelines and Reference Series, OECD Publishing, Paris, https://dx.doi.org/10.1787/9789264083905-en. [4]

OECD (2002), *Evaluation and Aid Effectiveness No. 6 - Glossary of Key Terms in Evaluation and Results Based Management (in English, French and Spanish)*, OECD Publishing, Paris, https://dx.doi.org/10.1787/9789264034921-en-fr. [2]

OECD (1991), *Principles for Evaluation of Development Assistance*, Development Assistance [1]
    Committee, OECD Publishing, Paris,
    https://www.oecd.org/development/evaluation/2755284.pdf (accessed on 11 January 2021).

Notes

[1] The document "Better criteria for better evaluation" (OECD, 2019[3]) provides a detailed explanation of changes made to the original definitions and justification for these modifications.

[2] A summary of the consultation findings is available on the EvalNet website: oe.cd/criteria

2 The six criteria: Their purpose and role within evaluation

This chapter outlines the purpose of the six evaluation criteria and explores their role within evaluation. It explains how the criteria can be thought of as a set of complementary lenses and the way that each criterion can provide a different perspective on the intervention and its results. The chapter also considers different types of interventions that can be evaluated by applying the criteria as the basis for judging its value or merit. The final section explores how the criteria relate to other evaluation norms and standards.

What is a criterion?

A criterion is a standard or principle used in evaluation as the basis for evaluative judgement.

Each of the six criteria is summarised by a broad question, which illustrates its overall meaning. Each one represents an important element for consideration:

- Relevance: Is the intervention[1] doing the right things?
- Coherence: How well does the intervention fit?
- Effectiveness: Is the intervention achieving its objectives?
- Efficiency: How well are resources being used?
- Impact: What difference does the intervention make?
- Sustainability: Will the benefits last?

The evaluation criteria's purpose is to support consistent, high-quality evaluation within a common framework. They provide a normative framework with which to assess a specific intervention. The criteria can also be used in processes beyond evaluation, including defining frameworks and indicators for monitoring and results management, funding approval, strategic planning and intervention design, particularly to improve future interventions. Collectively, there is value in having commonly defined criteria that are similarly applied across interventions. The criteria also provide a consistent language across the development field, providing standardisation and allowing for comparison and learning across interventions.

The criteria should be viewed as a set of lenses through which one can understand and analyse an intervention. The criteria provide complementary perspectives, giving a holistic picture of the intervention. They encourage deeper thinking about the nature of an intervention, its implementation, process and results. Together they describe the desired attributes of interventions, make explicit assumptions and provide norms: that interventions should be relevant to the context, coherent with other interventions, achieve results in an efficient way and have positive, lasting impacts for sustainable development. The evaluation criteria also provide a widely accepted framework for developing an approach to evaluation, a comprehensive and systematic approach and a common language that is used from the very start of the evaluation process.

The criteria are related and can be seen as a complementary set, to which each criterion brings a different and unique perspective to the understanding of the intervention. The definition of each criterion presents a distinct concept (captured in the overarching question for each) and yet these concepts are in many ways interrelated. Development interventions are typically multifaceted so using the criteria relationally can help the evaluator to consider the intervention as a whole.

The evaluation criteria are not a methodology and they are not the goals that an intervention is trying to achieve. Instead they provide prompts for asking the right questions during the evaluation of an intervention. Every intervention (the object or evaluand[2]) is different, which is why the evaluation process needs to be flexible and the use of evaluation criteria should be thoughtful and adapted to the purpose and users. In accordance with evaluation quality standards, conclusions and recommendations about progress and performance should be based on appropriate, credible evidence. The logic, credibility and interpretation of evidence should be clear and follow the theory of change or logic of the intervention.

What types of interventions can be evaluated with these criteria?

The term "intervention" is used throughout the guidance to mean the topic or object of the evaluation. It encompasses all the different types of efforts that may be evaluated using these criteria. These can be either international or domestic, aiming to support sustainable development or humanitarian goals.

An intervention may denote a project, programme, policy, strategy, thematic area, technical assistance, policy advice, an institution, financing mechanism, instrument, or other activity. It includes development interventions, humanitarian assistance, peacebuilding support, normative work and other international co-operation activities, as well as the activities of private sector actors and national governments in domestic policy contexts. The criteria have been used, for example, to evaluate topics ranging from the efficiency of national school feeding programmes, to the coherence of international support provided by different actors in a conflict-affected region. They are also used to evaluate policies or strategies (e.g. see Box 2.1). Evaluations also use the criteria when evaluating a suite of interventions – for example an evaluation of various projects supporting the education sector or a single large "intervention" lasting many years and involving multiple partners (e.g. general budget support).

The term "intervention" is used in this document as it is the most easily understood, but evaluators should take care to define clearly the topic of the evaluation – the intervention being analysed – and the evaluation scope, early on in the process. Using other more specific words related to the intervention in question – such as project or policy – is likely to be more useful and more readily understood by partners.

Box 2.1. Adapting the criteria to the intervention: Evaluation of the BMZ's "Action Plan for the Inclusion of Persons with Disabilities"

The evaluation of the German Federal Ministry for Economic Co-operation and Development's (BMZ) Action Plan for Inclusion of Persons with Disabilities provides an interesting example of how the criteria may be adjusted to reflect the intervention being evaluated (in this case a strategic action plan) and how the criteria connect to the evaluation questions. The evaluation was designed to examine how successful the Action Plan had been in advancing the systematic mainstreaming of inclusion within German development co-operation. The evaluation was based on the following general evaluation questions, which were drawn from the Action Plan itself. Each of these general questions was broken down into more detailed questions by criteria:

1. To what extent does the BMZ set a good example in its own organisation with regard to the inclusion of persons with disabilities?

- Relevance: To what extent do the selected fields of action and measures correspond to the provisions of the United Nations Convention on the Rights of Persons with Disabilities (CRPD)?
- Effectiveness: To what extent is BMZ succeeding in establishing inclusive structures and practices?

2. To what extent does the Action Plan help boost the inclusion of persons with disabilities in the partner countries of German development co-operation?

- Relevance: To what extent do the selected fields of action and measures correspond to the provisions of the CRPD?
- Effectiveness: To what extent were persons with disabilities included more effectively in measures in the partner countries of German development co-operation?

3. To what extent does the BMZ act at the national, regional and international levels as an advocate and partner for the rights of persons with disabilities in development co-operation?

- Relevance: To what extent do the selected fields of action and measures correspond to the provisions of the United Nations CRPD?
- Effectiveness: To what extent has the BMZ succeeded in winning over bilateral and multilateral actors to the cause of inclusion?

4. How was the development and implementation of the Action Plan for Inclusion managed?

- Effectiveness: Which management mechanisms and structures (including the roles of the various stakeholder groups in the management process) determined the development and implementation of the Action Plan?

- Efficiency: To what extent were the measures implemented as planned?

5. How should we rate the benefits of the Action Plan for Inclusion in terms of its breadth of impact and leverage as a governance instrument?

- Impact: To what extent did the Action Plan generate broad impact?

- Impact: To what overall extent did the Action Plan create leverage?

Source: Schwedersky, Ahrens and Steckhan (2017[1]), *Evaluation of the BMZ Action Plan for the Inclusion of Persons with Disabilities*, https://d-nb.info/1186644206/34

Where do the criteria fit in to the broader evaluation field?

Because every intervention (the entity being evaluated) is different, the evaluation process needs to be flexible and the use of evaluation criteria should be thoughtful and adapted to the purpose and users. The purpose of the criteria is not therefore to provide a mandatory set of rules.

The criteria do not exist in isolation. To make best use of the criteria it is important to understand where they fit in relation to other norms and standards, methodologies and institution-level guidance.

- The macro level is where the core principles for evaluation are situated, such as impartiality and independence, credibility, usefulness and participation (OECD, 1991[2]) along with the *Quality Standards for Development Evaluation* (OECD, 2010[3]). This level also includes the ethical standards related to research and data collection. These provide the overarching standards for good practice that all evaluations should adhere to throughout the process.

- The evaluation criteria are found at a meso level, providing the lenses through which the intervention is analysed and understood.

- The institutional level is where each organisation adapts the criteria and translates them into their own guidelines and policies (e.g. emphasising certain criteria, mandating ratings, adding additional criteria), reflecting their own mandates and priorities.

- The micro level, i.e. within the context of each individual evaluation, includes the decisions about the evaluation questions and methodologies that are employed for each evaluation, and how the criteria are applied in that context and to that specific evaluand.

Figure 2.1. How the criteria fit in with other norms and standards

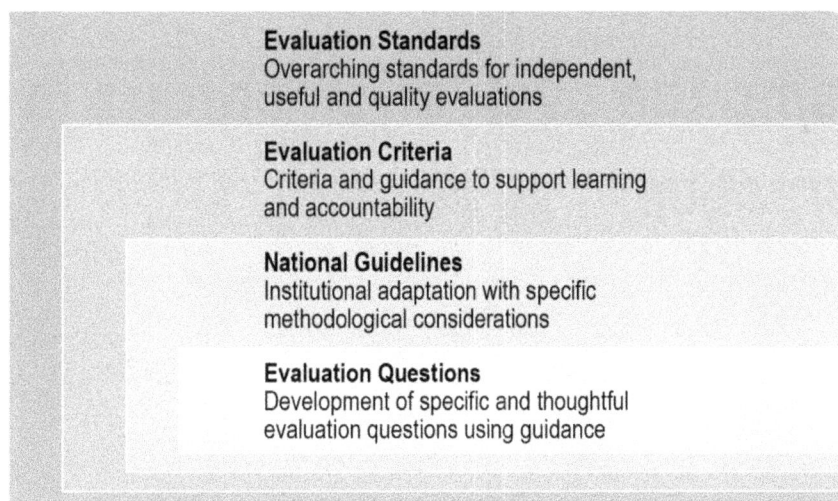

Evaluation Standards
Overarching standards for independent,
useful and quality evaluations

Evaluation Criteria
Criteria and guidance to support learning
and accountability

National Guidelines
Institutional adaptation with specific
methodological considerations

Evaluation Questions
Development of specific and thoughtful
evaluation questions using guidance

References

OECD (2010), *Quality Standards for Development Evaluation*, DAC Guidelines and Reference [3]
Series, OECD Publishing, Paris, https://dx.doi.org/10.1787/9789264083905-en.

OECD (1991), *Principles for Evaluation of Development Assistance*, Development Assistance [2]
Committee, OECD Publishing, Paris,
https://www.oecd.org/development/evaluation/2755284.pdf (accessed on 11 January 2021).

Schwedersky, T., L. Ahrens and H. Steckhan (2017), *Evaluation of the BMZ Action Plan for the* [1]
Inclusion of Persons with Disabilities, DEval, https://d-nb.info/1186644206/34 (accessed on
11 January 2021).

Notes

[1] The term "intervention" is used here and throughout the document to mean the object of the evaluation (the thing that is being evaluated). See chapter 3.2, Adapting the criteria to the evaluation's purpose, for further discussion on this point.

[2] The term "evaluand" refers to the object of the evaluation – the thing that is being evaluated.

3 Using the evaluation criteria in practice

This chapter considers the practical aspects of how the criteria should be used in evaluation design and implementation. It reviews the two main principles that should guide the application of the criteria. The chapter begins by exploring different approaches that can support thoughtful application of the criteria. It then addresses how the criteria can be applied within different institutional settings with different strategic priorities, ways of working and cultures. It outlines how the criteria can prompt evaluators to consider differential experiences and impacts by applying a gender lens. Finally, it examines how the criteria can help evaluators and evaluation managers to work in ways that support achievement of the Sustainable Development Goals and the wider 2030 Agenda. The chapter includes a range of practical examples illustrating how the criteria have been applied to various evaluations.

To support evaluators and those involved in designing or managing interventions in developing evaluations that are helpful and appropriate to different contexts and stakeholders, the following two principles have been developed to guide their use. To avoid that the criteria are applied in ways that are mechanistic – discouraging critical thinking, creativity and ownership of participants – these principles should accompany the criteria whenever they are used (OECD, 2019[1]):

- **Principle One**: The criteria should be applied thoughtfully to support high-quality, useful evaluation.
- **Principle Two**: Use of the criteria depends on the purpose of the evaluation.

The following section elaborates on these two principles and outlines additional key concepts for working with the criteria, including how to adjust the criteria to specific contexts, how to examine the criteria at different moments in time, and how the criteria relate to one another.

Applying criteria thoughtfully

Principle one stresses that the criteria should be used thoughtfully. In practice, this means thinking critically about which criteria are most useful to support high-quality, useful evaluation that will be valuable to the intended users. Box 3.1 provides an example of how the criteria can be applied thoughtfully when evaluating an intervention.

Considering the following six aspects and their related questions will assist evaluators in the thoughtful application of the criteria:

- **Context**: What is the context of the intervention itself and how can the criteria be understood in the context of the individual evaluation, the intervention and the stakeholders?
- **Purpose**: What is the evaluation trying to achieve and what questions are most useful in pursuing and fulfilling this purpose?
- **Roles and power dynamics:** Who are the stakeholders, what are their respective needs and interests? What are the power dynamics between them? Who needs to be involved in deciding which criteria to apply and how to understand them in the local context? This could include questions about ownership and who decides what is evaluated and prioritised.
- **Intervention (evaluand)**: What type of intervention is being evaluated (a project, policy, strategy, sector)? What is its scope and nature? How direct or indirect are its expected results? What complex systems thinking are at play?
- **Evaluability**: Are there any constraints in terms of access, resources and data (including disaggregated data) impacting the evaluation, and how does this affect the criteria?
- **Timing**: At which stage of the intervention's lifecycle will the evaluation be conducted? Has the context in which the intervention is operating changed over time and if so, how? Should these changes be considered during the evaluation? The timing will influence the use of the criteria as well as the source of evidence.

> **Box 3.1. Thoughtful use of the criteria: Evaluation of Norway's civil society grant for developing countries**
>
> This evaluation examined the Norwegian civil society grant, which aims to strengthen civil society in developing countries and thus contribute to a stronger civil society with the ability and capacity to promote democratisation, improve human rights and reduce poverty.
>
> This evaluation applied the criteria in a "thoughtful" and flexible manner, interpreting them in a specific way reflecting the nature of the intervention (partnerships and capacity building with civil society organisations) and taking into account Norwegian priorities and the context. The evaluation uses the following criteria, adapted in certain respects:
>
> - impact – defined in relation to key outcomes such as democracy, income opportunities leading to reduced poverty
> - relevance – no changes
> - effectiveness – here defined in relation to the specific objectives of the partnership (i.e. service delivery, advocacy and capacity strengthening). Includes some mid-term outcomes such as creating space for civil society
> - sustainability – no changes.
>
> An additional criterion – "value added" – is also used. This is defined as professional competence, organisational and financial competence, and networking competence. It relates to issues that, in other contexts, might be covered under the criteria of effectiveness and efficiency.
>
> Source: Helle et al. (2018[2]), *From Donors to Partners? Evaluation of Norwegian Support to Strengthen Civil Society in Developing Countries through Norwegian Civil Society Organisations*, https://www.norad.no/globalassets/filer-2017/evaluering/1.18-from-donor-to-partners/1.18-from-donors-to-partners_main-report.pdf

Adapting the criteria to the evaluation's purpose

The most important aspect of deciding how to use the criteria is relating them to the aim of the evaluation and its context and then building the evaluation criteria and questions around this purpose. Box 3.2 gives two examples of how the purpose of an evaluation can be defined.

The criteria are not intended to be applied in a standard, fixed way for every intervention or used in a tick-box fashion. Indeed the criteria should be carefully interpreted or understood in relation to the intervention being evaluated. This encourages flexibility and adaptation of the criteria to each individual evaluation. It should be clarified which specific concepts in the criteria will be drawn upon in the evaluation and why.

The purpose of the evaluation should be carefully and clearly defined. Stakeholders involved in the evaluation should be included at this stage to ensure that they understand the goal of the evaluation and how it will be used.

Key questions to look at when determining the purpose of the evaluation include:

1. What is the demand for an evaluation, who is the target audience and how will they use the findings?
2. What is feasible given the characteristics and context of the intervention?
3. What degree of certainty is needed when answering the key questions?
4. When is the information needed?

5. What is already known about the intervention and its results? Who has this knowledge and how are they using it?

Quality and ethical standards should inform subsequent thinking about methodological approaches, design, implementation and management of the evaluation process.

When adjusting the criteria to a specific evaluation, it is also important to delve into causality and gauge the extent to which the evaluation will be able to attribute effects to the intervention being assessed. These considerations can help manage stakeholder expectations and determine which criteria will be covered in depth. This is most crucial for effectiveness and impact which is discussed in both sections below, but it is also indirectly applicable to, and may feed into, other criteria. For example, efficiency and sustainability could use the actual (or projected) benefits attributed to the intervention as assessed under effectiveness and impact. An evaluability analysis is a useful tool to check that the purpose is understood in depth.[1] Further explanation on how to interpret each criterion is covered in Chapter 4.

Box 3.2. Defining the purpose of the evaluation: Examples from Uganda, Kenya and Sweden

The Danish International Development Agency's (Danida) evaluation of water, sanitation and environment programmes in Uganda

The Evaluation Department of the Danish Ministry of Foreign Affairs commissioned an independent evaluation of Danish initiatives to improve water, sanitation and environment in Uganda over the period 1990-2017.

The evaluation's objectives were:

- to document the results and achievements in the sub-sectors
- to analyse the "value added" from Danida's support to the sub-sectors
- to extract lessons learned.

To those ends, the evaluation focused on assessing effectiveness in two stages: 1) at the sector and cross-cutting level, and 2) at sub-sector level. The evaluation also assessed the value of the initiatives and looked at the sustainability of these results.

United Nations High Commissioner for Refugees (UNHCR) and Denmark joint evaluation

The joint evaluation by the UNHCR and Denmark of the refugee response in and around Kalobeyei, Kenya, defines the purpose in the following way:

> "The main purpose of the evaluation is to contribute to learning about the integrated settlement model in and around Kalobeyei. By documenting lessons learned from a concrete effort to link humanitarian and long-term development assistance, the intention is to provide evidence of the potentials and challenges of designing and implementing an integrated solutions model."

Evaluation of the Swedish International Development Cooperation Agency's (Sida) support to peacebuilding in conflict and post-conflict contexts

The evaluation report gives a useful example of how the evaluation reflects the purpose. It gives the following explanation:

The purpose or intended use of the evaluation is to systematise lessons learned from peacebuilding practice. The evaluation will serve as an input to the process of conceptualising and developing the peacebuilding approach used by the Swedish International Development Cooperation Agency (Sida). These approaches will in turn influence strategic planning and design of future Sida support in contexts

---

affected by conflict. Moreover, the evaluation is expected to contribute to increased understanding of peacebuilding as a concept and practice.

The specific objective of the evaluation was to evaluate how Sida has approached peacebuilding on the strategic level in different contexts. To that end, the evaluation paid particular attention to four of the criteria:

- relevance of Sida's peacebuilding work vis-à-vis contextual and beneficiary needs, and Sida's policy priorities
- effectiveness of its peacebuilding work in terms of contributing to overall peacebuilding objectives and its ability to provide a conducive framework for its partners' peacebuilding work
- impact of its peacebuilding work
- sustainability of its peacebuilding work.

Across all four criteria, special emphasis was given to results related to gender equality, female empowerment and rights, as well as inclusiveness of marginalised groups and ethnic minorities. For all four case study countries, the evaluations focused on aspects of marginalisation that were linked to peacebuilding and which have appeared in the literature and interviews. Marginalised groups were primarily considered from the perspective of ethnicity or as a consequence of being a minority. This is because, in all four cases, ethnic factors formed a major part of the root causes of conflict.

Sources: Danida (2019[3]), *Evaluation of Water, Sanitation and Environment Programmes in Uganda (1990-2017)*, http://www.oecd.org/derec/denmark/denmark-1990-2017-wash-environment-uganda.pdf;
ADE (2019[4]), *Joint Evaluation of the Integrated Solutions Model in and around Kalobeyei, Turkana, Kenya*, https://um.dk/en/danida-en/results/eval/eval_reports/publicationdisplaypage/?publicationid=dd54bef1-1152-468c-974b-c171fbc2452d;
Bryld (2019[5]), *Evaluation of Sida's Support to Peacebuilding in Conflict and Post-Conflict Contexts: Somalia Country Report*, https://publikationer.sida.se/contentassets/1396a7eb4f934e6b88e491e665cf57c1/eva2019_5_62214en.pdf

Understanding the time dimension

The criteria can be applied to different points in time. Each of the criteria can be used to evaluate before, during, or after an intervention. Likewise, they can be assessed during different moments in the intervention's lifecycle. However, the interpretation of the criteria and sources of evidence may be different at different points in time. For example, before an intervention has taken place, effectiveness and sustainability would be projections; whereas after the intervention, more data will be available from which to draw more solid conclusions.

The criteria – and related evaluation questions – should therefore reflect the following two key aspects related to timing: 1) the point in the lifecycle of the intervention when the evaluation will take place; and 2) the stage of the intervention or point of the result chain on which the evaluation will focus.

The conceptual frame of each criterion does not change if an evaluation is taking place before, during or after an intervention. However, the data and evidence available to *assess* the criteria and the methods used do change. Evaluators should keep these differences in mind when discussing the (potential) findings with evaluation stakeholders as this may influence the perceived usefulness and credibility of the evaluation. For example, an ex-ante evaluation of sustainability (taking place before the intervention begins) could look at the likelihood of an intervention's benefits continuing by examining the intervention design and available evidence on the validity of the assumptions about the continuation of expected benefits. After the completion of the intervention, an evaluation of sustainability would look at whether or not the benefits did in fact continue, this time drawing on data and evidence from the intervention's actual achieved benefits.

When looking back in time, evaluations will have to take into account the context and data available at that time so as to make judgements based on reasonable expectations of what could or should have been done. It would be unfair to judge the actions of past programme designers based on information available today that was not known to them at the time. However, many evaluations have found that available information was not fully utilised (where it could have been), which would have made the intervention more relevant. For example, local people were not sufficiently consulted and involved in the design of the intervention. Such an oversight could reasonably have been expected to be avoided and should therefore be flagged in an evaluation.

Using the criteria for better evaluation questions

Formulating good evaluation questions is a key part of the evaluation process and the use of the six criteria interacts with and supports the process of deciding on evaluation questions.[2] The process starts with a reflection on the purpose of the evaluation, how it will be used and by whom. An effective engagement with stakeholders through a well-designed participatory process can help evaluators and managers understand how they will use the evaluation. A deep understanding of the intervention and its context, its objectives and theory of change should complement this discussion with stakeholders. An inception phase can be used to explore these questions and generate (a small number of) key questions that the evaluation needs to address.

Following this initial step, the evaluation criteria then provide a tool for checking from different perspectives to see if anything has been missed, enabling further development and refining of the questions, which are essential to the evaluation design. This makes the process systematic and ensures that the evaluation is comprehensive. It is a crucial part of what constitutes a "better evaluation". It is highly recommended that this question development phase be undertaken with a clear and coherent overall approach.

The institution commissioning the evaluation may have taken a particular decision to evaluate interventions according to certain criteria. In this instance, the institutional guidance should be followed alongside thoughtful application of the criteria to ensure consistency.

An example of this is the Sida's evaluation manual, which provides examples of standard questions under each of the criteria (Molund and Schill, 2004[6]). Other examples of how institutions interpret and unpack the criteria are available, such as the guidance and technical notes that have been developed for evaluation managers and evaluators at the World Food Programme (WFP, 2016[7]).

Relationships between the criteria

The criteria comprise multiple lenses through which an intervention and its results can be viewed. They are interrelated, in that the concepts underpinning each one help to analyse complementary dimensions of the process of achieving results. For instance, effectiveness and impact look at different levels of the results chain, depending on how the objectives of the intervention have been defined. The two criteria are therefore interrelated along the causal chain.

The criteria often depend on each other. For example, an intervention that was not relevant to the priorities of the beneficiaries is unlikely to have the intended impact (unless there are some rather unusual separate channels of impact). An intervention that is poorly implemented (less effective) is also likely to be less sustainable. On the other hand, it is also possible that an intervention could be highly relevant yet ineffective. Or a highly coherent intervention could be very inefficient due to increased transaction costs. Evaluators should explore and reflect on relationships and synergies between different criteria, including considering if and how they are causally related.

Most evaluations draw conclusions based on the findings for each criterion, as well as an overall conclusion based on all criteria, sometimes using a numerical score to rate performance. In drawing conclusions about the intervention, and depending on the purpose of the assessment, evaluators should look at the full picture and consider how to appropriately weight all of the applied criteria. Criteria may be weighted with some institutions defining a dominant ("knock out") criterion. If performance is not satisfactory on that criterion, no matter how well other criteria scored, the intervention will be considered unsuccessful (or if *ex ante*, would not be funded).

More specific linkages between each criterion are discussed in Chapter 4.

Choosing which criteria to use

As described above, the purpose, priorities, scope and context of the intervention and the evaluation will shape the relative focus on different criteria. Evaluators should consider the relative value each criterion will add. This would include two basic decisions: Is this criterion an important consideration for this evaluation? Is it feasible to answer questions about this criterion?

While users may be tempted to simply apply all six criteria regardless of context, the better approach (i.e. the one that is consistent with the original intent of the criteria and that leads to the highest quality evaluation) is that of deliberately selecting and using the criteria in ways that are appropriate to the evaluation and to the questions that the evaluation is seeking to answer.

To achieve this, ask questions such as:

- If we could only ask one question about this intervention, what would it be?
- Which questions are best addressed through an evaluation and which might be addressed through other means (such as a research project, evidence synthesis, monitoring exercise or facilitated learning process)?
- Are the available data sufficient to provide a satisfying answer to this question? If not, will better or more data be available later?
- Who has provided input to the list of questions? Are there any important perspectives missing?
- Do we have sufficient time and resources to adequately address all of the criteria of interest, or will focusing the analysis on just some of the criteria provide more valuable information?

It is important to strike a balance between flexibility (avoiding a mechanistic application of all the criteria) and cherry-picking (selecting only the easiest criteria, or those that are likely to generate positive results) when using the criteria. Notably, one should not shy away from answering critical questions on impact and coherence, even though these questions can be more challenging at times. Some points for consideration are shown in Figure 3.1 below; it should be noted that these are examples and not a comprehensive checklist.

Figure 3.1. Considering how to cover the criteria for a specific evaluation

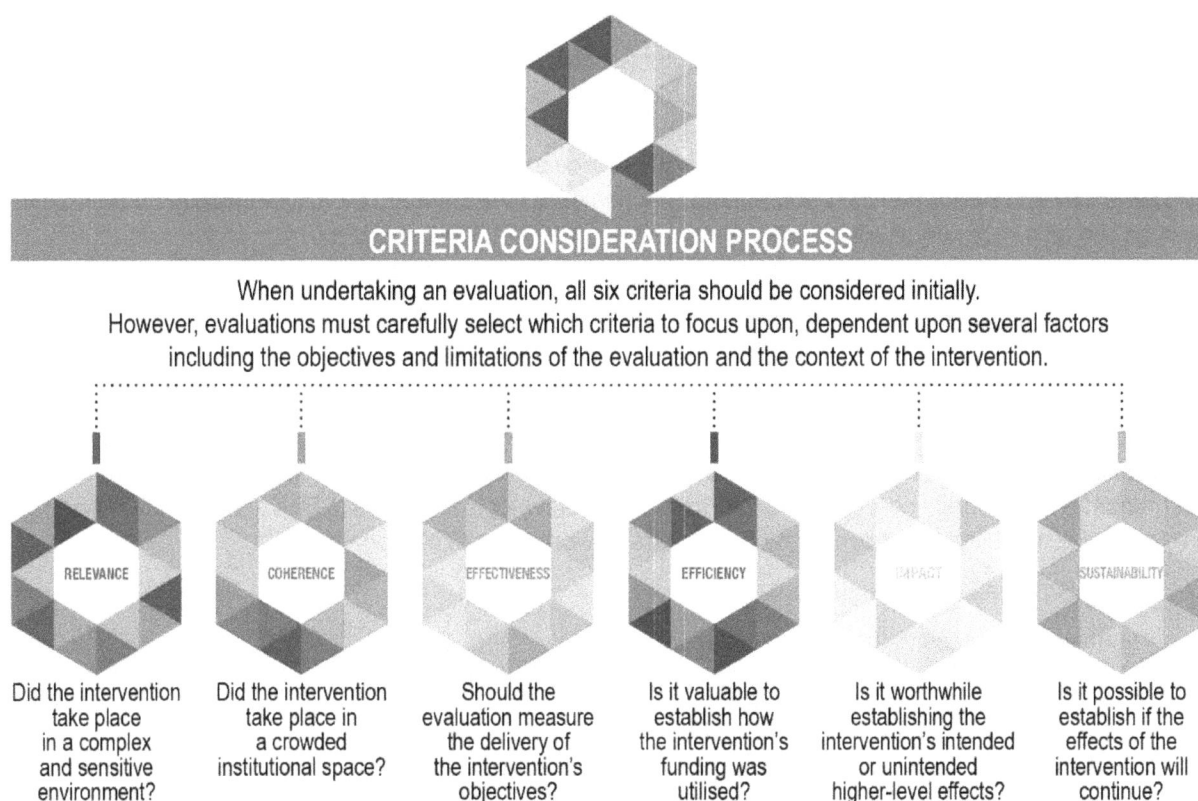

CRITERIA CONSIDERATION PROCESS

When undertaking an evaluation, all six criteria should be considered initially.
However, evaluations must carefully select which criteria to focus upon, dependent upon several factors including the objectives and limitations of the evaluation and the context of the intervention.

RELEVANCE	COHERENCE	EFFECTIVENESS	EFFICIENCY	IMPACT	SUSTAINABILITY
Did the intervention take place in a complex and sensitive environment?	Did the intervention take place in a crowded institutional space?	Should the evaluation measure the delivery of the intervention's objectives?	Is it valuable to establish how the intervention's funding was utilised?	Is it worthwhile establishing the intervention's intended or unintended higher-level effects?	Is it possible to establish if the effects of the intervention will continue?

A good knowledge of the stakeholders involved – in both the intervention and the evaluation – can help identify potential tensions between their different interests and priorities when it comes to the design and implementation of the evaluation. Beneficiaries may be most interested in understanding effectiveness (e.g. whether their children's health is improving through participation in a malnutrition treatment programme) while implementers may be more interested in understanding efficiency, with an eye to scaling up treatment to more families. In most cases, not all potentially interesting questions can be answered in a single evaluation and choices will have to be made. To increase the likelihood that questions that are left out of the evaluation will be covered elsewhere, it is good practice to document the process and outcomes of discussions about prioritising different stakeholder needs and deciding on evaluation questions.

Operationalising and adapting the criteria at an institutional level

The criteria definitions and this guidance provide a common platform and set of agreed definitions on which to build. However, tailoring them to the institutional context is crucial. Evaluators and evaluation managers often use the criteria on behalf of a development organisation, ministry, or other institution that has its own specific mandate, policy priorities, evaluation policy, standards and guidance – all as decided by their governing bodies.

When considering how to operationalise and apply the criteria, it is important that evaluators and commissioners carefully consider the organisation's strategic priorities, culture and opportunities as a background to decision making. The way certain terms – such as impact – are used varies, and it is important to pay close attention to the potential for confusion or misinterpretation of the criteria and their intended focus. This will assist evaluators and commissioners as they apply the criteria, maximise the use of the evaluation's findings and enhance relevance to the intended user's needs. Managers should encourage discussion between evaluators, commissioners and the target audience of the evaluation to consider how the criteria should be applied and interpreted. Such a process can support the design of credible and timely evaluations that better meet the users' needs.

Methodological requirements set by an institution may also have a bearing on how the criteria are applied. Evaluators should refer to the specific requirements and guidance of their own organisation or commissioner. Other relevant sources such as the United Nations Evaluation Group (UNEG) guidance or the Evaluation Co-operation Group's (ECG) good practice standards and the Active Learning Network for Accountability and Performance in Humanitarian Action's (ALNAP) guidance on evaluation in humanitarian settings are also very useful where applicable.

Responding to the 2030 Agenda and the Sustainable Development Goals

Along with adapting the criteria to the institutions in which they are being used, the way the criteria are understood and applied will reflect the broader policy context, influencing how evaluation managers, evaluators and stakeholders use the criteria. For the next decade, particularly for evaluators working in international development co-operation, the Sustainable Development Goals (SDGs) and the 2030 Agenda are the single most important overarching policy framework and set of global goals.

Key elements of the 2030 Agenda, include:

- universal access to the benefits of development
- inclusiveness, particularly for those at greatest risk of being left behind
- human rights, gender equality and other equity considerations
- environmental sustainability, climate change and natural resource management
- complexity of context and of development interventions
- synergies among actors engaged in the development process.

This framework influences both interventions and their evaluation, including how the criteria are interpreted as well as the process of evaluation itself (including who is involved in applying the criteria, identifying priority questions). Box 3.3 provides guidance for using the 2030 Agenda to inform national evaluation agendas. Box 3.4 gives an example of how this was done in the German development evaluation system (BMZ, 2020[8]). Similar efforts have been made by several national governments – including Costa Rica, Nigeria, Finland – and non-governmental organisations (NGOs) and provide useful lessons for evaluators and evaluation managers (D'Errico, Geoghe and Piergallini, 2020[9]).

The revised wording of the criteria definitions also reflect these elements in several ways. For example, by giving particular consideration to context and beneficiary perspectives and priorities when looking at relevance, effectiveness and impact; by taking account of equity of results under effectiveness and impact; and by adopting an integrated approach when looking at coherence. The guiding principles also reflect the 2030 Agenda by encouraging an integrated way of thinking.

Box 3.3. Using the SDGs to inform national evaluation agendas

"Evaluation to connect national priorities with the SDGs. A guide for evaluation commissioners and managers", outlines five considerations to support countries in developing evaluation agendas and enhancing the value of evaluation. Evaluators are encouraged to apply "complex systems thinking" and:

- think beyond single policies, programmes and projects
- examine macro forces influencing success or failure
- have a nuanced understanding of 'success'
- recognise the importance of culture
- adopt evaluative thinking and adaptive management

Source: Ofir et al. (2016[10]), *Briefing: Five considerations for national evaluation agendas informed by the SDGs*, https://pubs.iied.org/sites/default/files/pdfs/migrate/17374IIED.pdf

Box 3.4. Mapping the criteria to the 2030 Agenda and the SDGs

The following questions have been developed by the German Federal Ministry for Economic Co-operation and Development (BMZ) with the support of the German Institute for Development Evaluation (DEval) to help evaluators assess overall contributions to the 2030 Agenda and the SDGs. Each question below is a response to the SDG principles and also relates to the criteria.

Universality, shared responsibility and accountability

- To what extent does the intervention contribute to achieving the SDGs? (see impact criterion)
- To what extent is the intervention designed to use existing systems and structures (of partners/other donors/international organisations) for the implementation of their activities and to what extent are these used? (see coherence criterion)
- Is division of labour with other donors and development partners used when implementing the intervention? If so, to what extent? (see coherence criterion)
- To what extent are common systems used for monitoring, learning and accountability? (see coherence criterion)

Interaction of economic, environmental and social development

- To what extent does the intervention follow a holistic approach to sustainable development (social, environmental and economic)? (see relevance criterion)
- To what extent were there intended or unintended positive or negative interactions between the social, economic and environmental outcomes and what was the overall impact of the intervention? (see effectiveness and impact criterion)
- What contribution did the intervention make to promoting intended or unintended positive or negative interactions between the social, economic and environmental outcomes and what was the overall impact of the intervention? (see effectiveness and impact criterion)

Inclusiveness

- To what extent is the intervention consistent with international norms and standards on the participation and promotion of particularly disadvantaged and vulnerable groups? (see coherence criterion)

- To what extent were there intended or unintended positive or negative overarching developmental changes at the level of particularly disadvantaged and vulnerable groups (possible differentiation according to age, income, gender, ethnicity, etc.)? (see impact criterion)

- What contribution did the intervention make to the intended or unintended positive or negative overarching developmental impacts at the level of particularly disadvantaged and vulnerable groups (possible differentiation according to age, income, gender, ethnicity, etc.)? (see impact criterion)

- To what extent did the intervention contribute to strengthening the resilience of particularly disadvantaged or vulnerable groups (possible differentiation according to age, income, gender, ethnicity, etc.)? (see sustainability criterion)

Source: BMZ (2020[8]), *Evaluation Criteria for German Bilateral Development Co-operation*

Applying a gender lens to the criteria

Evaluators should work in ways that thoughtfully consider differential experiences and impacts by gender, and the way they interact with other forms of discrimination in a specific context (e.g. age, race and ethnicity, social status). Regardless of the intervention, evaluators should consider how power dynamics based on gender intersect and interact with other forms of discrimination to affect the intervention's implementation and results. This may involve exploring how the political economy and socio-cultural context of interventions influence delivery and the achievement of objectives.

Applying a gender lens can provide evidence for learning and accountability while supporting the achievement of gender equality goals. Practical steps to apply a gender lens to the evaluation criteria include:

- evaluators, managers, and commissioners working in ways that are inclusive and lead to appropriate participation in decision making, data collection, analysis and sharing of findings
- considering the extent to which gender interacts with other social barriers to jeopardise equal opportunity in the intervention
- considering how an intervention interacts with the legislative, economic, political, religious and socio-cultural environment to better interpret different stakeholder experiences and impacts
- considering socially constructed definitions of masculinity, femininity and any changes to gender dynamics and roles
- analysis of evaluator skills in gender-sensitive evaluation approaches and experiences of working in different contexts when selecting evaluators.

The following table has been developed to help evaluators to reflect on how they can apply a gender lens to the criteria:

Table 3.1. Applying a gender lens to the criteria

Criteria	Guiding questions for applying a gender lens
Relevance	Was the intervention designed in ways that respond to the needs and priorities of all genders? If so, how?
	To what extent does the intervention's design reflect the rights of persons of all genders and include feedback from a diverse range of local stakeholders including marginalised groups?
	Does the intervention meet the practical and strategic needs of all genders?
Coherence	To what extent are the intervention's design, delivery and results coherent with international laws and commitments to gender equality and rights, including the Convention on the Elimination of All Forms of Discrimination Against Women (CEDAW), the Beijing Declaration and Platform for Action, the Programme of Action of the International Conference on Population and Development, and the 2030 Agenda?
	To what extent does the intervention support national legislation and initiatives that aim to improve gender equality and human rights? What lessons can be learned?
Effectiveness	Did the intervention achieve its objectives and expected results in ways that contribute to gender equality? If so, how?
	Were there differential results for different people? If so, how and why? Were different approaches necessary to reach people of different genders? Was there sufficient monitoring and analysis of differential effects? Was the intervention adjusted to address any concerns and maximise effectiveness?
	Was the theory of change and results framework informed by analysis of gender equality, political economy analysis and human rights? If so, to what extent?
	To what extent and why is effectiveness different for people of different genders?
Efficiency	Were different resources allocated in ways that considered gender equality? If so, how were they allocated? Was differential resource allocation appropriate?
	Do the investment costs per person targeted meet the differentiated needs of people of different genders?
Impact	Were there equal impacts for different genders or were there any gender-related differences in engagement, experience and impacts? If so, why did these differential impacts occur?
	To what extent did gender-related impacts intersect with other social barriers including race/ethnicity, disability, age and sexual orientation to contribute to differential experiences and outcomes?
	How did gendered norms and barriers within the wider political, economic, religious, legislative and socio-cultural environment impact outcomes?
	To what extent have impacts contributed to equal power relations between people of different genders and to changing of social norms and systems?
Sustainability	Did the intervention contribute to greater gender equality within wider legal, political, economic and social systems? If so, how and to what extent? Did it result in enduring changes to social norms that are harmful to people of all or some genders? If it did not achieve this, why not?
	Will the achievements in gender equality persist after the conclusion of the intervention? Have processes contributed to sustaining these benefits? Have mechanisms been set up to support the achievement of gender equality in the longer term?

Using other criteria

The six criteria are intended to be a complete set that fully reflects all important concepts to be covered in evaluations. If applied thoughtfully and in contextually relevant ways they will be adequate for evaluations across the sustainable development and humanitarian fields.

Nonetheless, in certain contexts, other criteria are used. For instance, in their evaluation policies many institutions will mandate analysis of a particular focus area. In 2020, an evaluation of Italy's health programmes in Bolivia used nine criteria: relevance, effectiveness, efficiency, impact, sustainability, coherence, added value of Italian co-operation, visibility of Italian co-operation and ownership (Eurecna Spa, 2020[11]). Another example involves applying the criteria to humanitarian situations, where criteria such as appropriateness, coverage and connectedness are highly relevant.[3] Additionality is a criterion that is sometimes applied, often in the fields of blended finance, non-sovereign finance and climate finance. Various definitions for additionality, including different types of financial and non-financial additionality, are used.[4] Depending on the definition used, additionality may be examined under the criterion of relevance, effectiveness or impact. Others treat it as a distinct cross-cutting criterion.

Users should be cautious when considering whether to add criteria, as this can lead to confusion and make an evaluation too broad (providing a less useful analysis). Having a limited number of criteria is useful for ensuring sufficient depth of analysis and conceptual clarity – a point that was repeatedly made during the consultation process when updating the definitions in 2017-2019.

When using other criteria, it is important to define them. An explanation of why they are being added can help ensure that other people understand how the additional criteria fit with the six described here. To support learning across evaluations, it is critical that the same concepts or elements are assessed under the same criteria.

Regardless of which criteria are used, the core principles and guidance provided here should be applied.

References

ADE (2019), *Joint Evaluation of the Integrated Solutions Model in and around Kalobeyei, Turkana, Kenya*, UNHCR and Danida, https://um.dk/en/danida-en/results/eval/eval_reports/publicationdisplaypage/?publicationid=dd54bef1-1152-468c-974b-c171fbc2452d (accessed on 11 January 2021). [4]

Bamberger, M., J. Vaessen and E. Raimondo (2015), *Dealing With Complexity in Development Evaluation - A Practical Approach*, https://www.betterevaluation.org/en/resources/dealing_with_complexity_in_development_evaluation (accessed on 11 January 2021). [12]

BMZ (2020), *Evaluation Criteria for German Bilateral Development Co-operation*. [8]

Bryld, E. (2019), *Evaluation of Sida's Support to Peacebuilding in Conflict and Post-Conflict Contexts: Somalia Country Report*, Sida, https://publikationer.sida.se/contentassets/1396a7eb4f934e6b88e491e665cf57c1/eva2019_5_62214en.pdf (accessed on 11 January 2021). [5]

D'Errico, S., T. Geoghe and I. Piergallini (2020), *Evaluation to connect national priorities with the SDGs | Publications Library*, IIED, https://pubs.iied.org/17739IIED (accessed on 22 February 2021). [9]

Danida (2019), *Evaluation of Water, Sanitation and Environment Programmes in Uganda (1990-2017)*, Evaluation Department, Ministry of Foreign Affairs of Denmark, http://www.oecd.org/derec/denmark/denmark-1990-2017-wash-environment-uganda.pdf (accessed on 11 January 2021). [3]

Davis, R. (2013), "Planning Evaluability Assessments: A Synthesis of the Literature with Recommendations", No. 40, DIFD, https://www.gov.uk/government/publications/planning-evaluability-assessments (accessed on 12 January 2021). [13]

Eurecna Spa (2020), *Bolivia - Evaluation of Health Initiatives (2009-2020)*, Italian Ministry of Foreign Affairs and International Cooperation, http://www.oecd.org/derec/italy/evaluation-report-of-health-initiatives-in-Bolivia-2009_2020.pdf (accessed on 11 January 2021). [11]

Helle, E. et al. (2018), *From Donors to Partners? Evaluation of Norwegian Support to Strengthen Civil Society in Developing Countries through Norwegian Civil Society Organisations*, Norad Norwegian Agency for Development Cooperation, https://www.norad.no/globalassets/filer-2017/evaluering/1.18-from-donor-to-partners/1.18-from-donors-to-partners_main-report.pdf (accessed on 11 January 2021). [2]

Molund, S. and G. Schill (2004), *Looking Back, Moving Forward Sida Evaluation Manual*, Sida, https://www.oecd.org/derec/sweden/35141712.pdf (accessed on 11 January 2021). [6]

OECD (2019), *Better Criteria for Better Evaluation: Revised Evaluation Criteria Definitions and Principles for Use*, DAC Network on Development Evaluation, OECD Publishing, Paris, https://www.oecd.org/dac/evaluation/revised-evaluation-criteria-dec-2019.pdf (accessed on 11 January 2021). [1]

OECD (2002), *Evaluation and Aid Effectiveness No. 6 - Glossary of Key Terms in Evaluation and Results Based Management (in English, French and Spanish)*, OECD Publishing, Paris, https://dx.doi.org/10.1787/9789264034921-en-fr. [14]

Ofir, Z. et al. (2016), *Briefing: Five considerations for national evaluation agendas informed by the SDGs*, IIED, London, http://dx.doi.org/10.3138/cjpe.30.3.02./11. [10]

WFP (2016), *Technical Note: Evaluation Methodology*, DEQAS, World Food Programme, https://docs.wfp.org/api/documents/704ec01f137d43378a445c7e52dcf324/download/ (accessed on 11 January 2021). [7]

Notes

[1] Evaluability is the extent to which an activity or a programme can be evaluated in a reliable and credible fashion. Evaluability assessment calls for the early review of a proposed activity in order to ascertain whether its objectives are adequately defined and its results verifiable (OECD, 2002[14]). See also Davis (2013[13]).

[2] The process of formulating evaluation questions and involving stakeholders, while also taking into account the complexity of the intervention is discussed in more detail by, for example, Bamberger, Vaessen and Raimondo (2015[12]).

[3] The Active Learning Network for Accountability and Performance in Humanitarian Action (ALNAP) is currently updating its 2006 guidance on using the criteria in humanitarian settings, as a compliment to ALNAP's comprehensive *Evaluation of Humanitarian Action Guide*.

[4] EvalNet's Working Group on Evaluating Blended Finance supported research on the definitions of additionality and related concepts. Findings will be published in early 2021.

4 Understanding the six criteria: Definitions, elements for analysis and key challenges

This chapter considers each of the six criteria in greater detail. It explores what their definition means in practice, different elements of analysis and how the criteria can be applied in ways that critically reflect inclusion and equality. For each criterion, a table outlines key challenges to their application with practical recommendations on how they can be addressed by evaluators and evaluation managers. The chapter includes a range of examples that illustrate the practical application of the criteria and prompt critical reflection on the dimensions of each definition.

This chapter introduces the six criteria (Figure 4.1), presenting them in the order in which they are most logically considered: starting with relevance and coherence, then effectiveness and efficiency, and finally impact and sustainability. Each criterion is defined and its importance described. Then the definition is further explained through an examination of its elements of analysis – the key concepts contained within the definition. These elements are not sub-criteria but illustrate the different ways the criteria can be applied according to the context and purpose. Connections with other criteria are also explored.

The chapter also includes initial thinking on key issues related to inclusion and the principle of "leaving no one behind", as mandated in the 2030 Agenda. Further work is underway to explore applying an equity lens to the criteria and evaluation approaches, including specific guidance on gender equality, women's empowerment and human rights.

For each of the criterion, a table outlines common challenges along with some ideas for evaluators and evaluation managers on overcoming these challenges. These tables will be updated over time as experiences with the new definitions are shared.

Finally, real world examples are provided to illustrate ways of interpreting each criterion.

Figure 4.1. The six criteria and their related questions

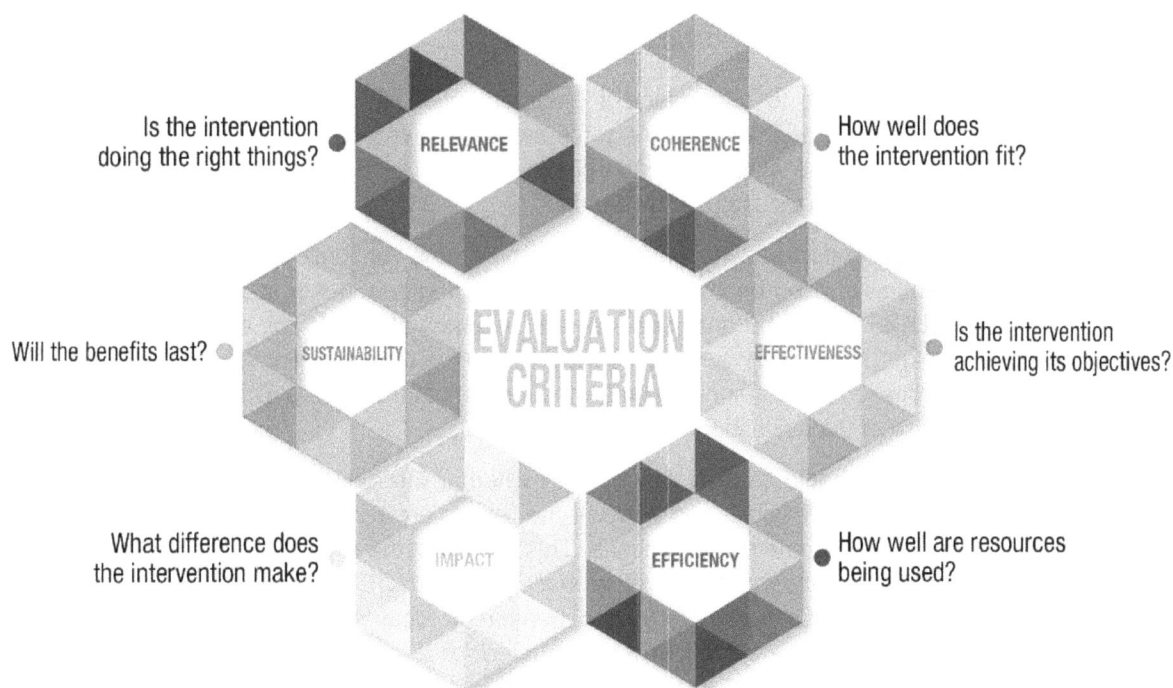

Definition of relevance:

Relevance: Is the intervention doing the right things?

The extent to which the intervention's objectives and design respond to beneficiaries'[1] global, country and partner/institution needs, policies and priorities, and continue to do so if circumstances change.

Note: "Respond to" means that the objectives and design of the intervention are sensitive to the economic, environmental, equity, social, political economy and capacity conditions in which it takes place. "Partner/institution" includes government (national, regional, local), civil society organisations, private entities and international bodies involved in funding, implementing and/or overseeing the intervention. Relevance assessment involves looking at differences and trade-offs between different priorities or needs. It requires analysing any changes in the context to assess the extent to which the intervention can be (or has been) adapted to remain relevant.

What is relevance and why is it important?

Evaluating relevance helps users to understand if an intervention is doing the right thing. It allows evaluators to assess how clearly an intervention's goals and implementation are aligned with beneficiary and stakeholder needs, and the priorities underpinning the intervention. It investigates if target stakeholders view the intervention as useful and valuable.

Relevance is a pertinent consideration across the programme or policy cycle from design to implementation. Relevance can also be considered in relation to global goals such as the Sustainable Development Goals (SDGs). It can be analysed via four potential elements for analysis: relevance to beneficiary and stakeholder needs, relevance to context, relevance of quality and design, and relevance over time. These are discussed in greater detail under the elements for analysis. They should be included as required by the purpose of the evaluation and are not exhaustive.

The evaluation of relevance should start by determining whether the objectives of the intervention are adequately defined, realistic and feasible, and whether the results are verifiable and aligned with current international standards for development interventions. This should fit the concept of evaluability, which is detailed in the *OECD's Quality Standards for Development Evaluation* (OECD, 2010[1]) Results or objective statements may be poorly phrased or vague, difficult to measure or focused on activities or inputs. In some cases the theory of change must be refined or reconstructed for the evaluator to clearly identify these objectives. Evaluators should take care to assess against good quality and realistic objectives. The indicators for measuring the achievement of the objectives should also be validated according to generally accepted criteria such as the SMART (Specific, Measurable, Attainable, Relevant and Timely) indicators (IDD and Associates, 2006[2]). Evaluations which consider relevance should consider if and how appropriate objectives have been operationalised in ways that reflect good practice. They should also reflect on the organisational capacity and capability of implementing partners and their responses to any change in context.

Evaluators should also clearly identify stakeholders whose needs and priorities should be considered during the evaluation of relevance. This includes beneficiaries, as well as funding, oversight or implementing partners and institutions. A particular emphasis should be placed on beneficiaries. Ownership of an intervention is important and beneficiaries are considered first and foremost to be the primary stakeholders in defining priorities and needs. Depending on the intervention, it may also be pertinent to consider national and sub-national (where applicable) needs, local strategies to address needs and the extent to which the intervention aligns with those needs. Institutional needs can include but are not limited to donor needs, meaning relevance can be evaluated across policy contexts including those where there is no clear donor but instead partners in an intervention (e.g. in the case of trade policy).

Understanding relevance: Elements for analysis

The definition of relevance comprises four main dimensions: responding to needs, policies and priorities; being sensitive and responsive to context; quality of design; and responsiveness over time.

Responding to needs, policies and priorities

Perhaps the most important element for analysing relevance is the assessment of the extent to which an intervention addresses beneficiaries' needs and priorities. This analysis provides insight into which issues an intervention addresses and why. Beneficiaries are central stakeholders for an intervention and should be considered throughout. Beneficiaries are not necessarily people receiving direct services. Depending on the type of intervention, beneficiaries can be (much) further upstream in the results chain. For example, an intervention may aim at increasing the capacity of a national audit office. These improved capacities will strengthen public financial management and ultimately contribute to achieving sustainable development goals such as improved health and education. But the beneficiaries for the purpose of evaluating the capacity support would focus on the audit office staff as the primary beneficiaries. Clearly defining the beneficiaries (primary and secondary) is a necessary first step to evaluating relevance.

Analysing beneficiaries' needs and whether they are addressed sheds light not only on responsiveness but also on ownership and participation regarding the intervention's design and implementation (which can affect other criteria). It helps to understand who is involved in the design and who is not and, in turn, how this affects the intervention's design and implementation.

This criterion implies that efforts should focus on areas of greatest need, or in the language of the 2030 Agenda: reaching the furthest behind first. Indeed, relevance is particularly useful in understanding who is engaged in and reached by an intervention. Relevance provides an opportunity for evaluators to consider whether and to what extent marginalised groups are incorporated in both policy and intervention priorities. Even when an intervention is perfectly in sync with official policy, it may be disconnected from the real life priorities of the participants, who may not have been involved in setting official priorities and plans.

An evaluation of relevance should also take into account how the intervention addresses the priorities of involved institutions or partners. This includes government (national, regional, local), civil society organisations, private entities and international bodies involved in funding, implementing and/or overseeing the intervention. Relevance will examine alignment with these institutions strategies and policies.

To assess an intervention's relevance to global needs, policies and priorities, an evaluation should review its contribution to overall global goals (i.e. the relative importance of this intervention compared to the broader effort). This will often involve evaluators comparing (potential) results in the context/country with alternatives elsewhere. Such questions regarding global relevance are not always examined during the intervention design. Evaluators can thus provide useful analysis on these questions to assist stakeholders in understanding the strategic significance of an intervention beyond its local context.

The definition of relevance also calls on evaluators to look at potential tensions or trade-offs with regard to whose needs and priorities are met through the intervention. Various perspectives of the participants and other stakeholders may be misaligned and so the evaluation will need to unpack these differences and explore the implications of choices made. To provide an example, interventions aimed at eliminating a disease – such as polio – from all countries would examine the relative disease burden to determine the global priority for action in a particular country or region. There may be cases where the global priority for that intervention (polio vaccinations in the last remaining region with community transmission) may be at odds with local priorities (with beneficiaries prioritising water and sanitation issues, for instance). It can be useful for the evaluators to unearth such tensions, through careful analysis of relevance.

Being sensitive and responsive to the context

The needs of beneficiaries and other key stakeholders cannot be understood in isolation and are shaped by their context. Context is multifaceted and includes the following factors: economic, environmental, equity, social, cultural, political economy and capacity considerations. Evaluators are encouraged to understand which contextual factors are most pertinent to an intervention.

Contextual relevance can be analysed both in intervention design and implementation. The consideration of context will also be dependent on whether an evaluation is *ex ante* or *ex post*. For example, evaluators can ask questions around how the context was understood and accounted for when the intervention was designed. For ex-post evaluations, evaluators should consider whether the context changed between the inception and the end of the intervention. Ex-post evaluations will have more context and should aim to incorporate this in their analysis. This complements the time element for analysis of the relevance criterion, by considering any fluctuations in the relevance of an intervention as circumstances change.

Historical context can also be considered. For example, have similar interventions occurred before? Are there historical tensions, legislation or politics that may impact the understanding of needs and shaping of goals? Historical context can also include assumptions that were made in the past about an intervention's relevance and test if these persist in the current context. Where previous evaluations have been conducted, these assumptions may be helpful in tracing the historical context and whether interventions capitalise on lessons learned from previous evaluation exercises.

Quality of design

"Quality of design" considers how well the intervention was built to address relevant priorities and needs and whether goals have been clearly specified. Moreover, it assesses if stakeholders' priorities and needs are articulated in the intervention's objectives, its underlying theory of change, theory of action and/or modus-operandi. This allows evaluators to understand gaps in programme design that may have undermined an intervention's overall relevance. This element for analysis also influences the evaluability of the overall intervention by adding a focus on the intervention's design quality at the outset. It also provides insight into the intervention's appropriateness to the institution implementing it. For example, evaluators can consider if it has been designed with technical, organisational and financial feasibility in mind.

Adapting over time

Evaluators should consider how interventions can evolve over time. Outbreaks of conflict, or changing policy and economic contexts, for example, will significantly affect implementation. Relevance regarding time considerations should include adaptive management analysis. Evaluators should consider relevance not only at the beginning and end of a programme, but how it has responded to changes over the course of its lifespan. This allows evaluators to examine any fluctuations in the relevance of an intervention as implementation conditions change. For example, this could include an analysis of how suitable the adaptations were in continuing to meet the most important needs and priorities and whether adaptation affected the quality of the design over time.

Again, ongoing adaptation to external contexts and internal changes should be taken into account (e.g. when a change in funding necessitates a change in programming). Additionally, risks and opportunities can be considered, including the extent to which the programme mitigated risks that would undermine its purpose, or was adapted to seize a good opportunity, or to better meet needs. Adaptation may lead to trade-offs in whose needs are prioritised, raising questions of accountability. This should be fully explored to understand how it may, or may not, have altered a programme's relevance.

Connections with other criteria

As the criteria are interrelated, relevance can be linked to other criteria in the evaluation. Relevance is often viewed as a prerequisite for achieving the other criteria.

- The evaluation of relevance provides a foundation to understand if needs are met as part of effectiveness and impact. Indeed, relevance as a criterion is a prerequisite for effectiveness as the identification of needs and goals must be clearly articulated to enable the assessment of effectiveness.

- Relevance complements coherence. Both require contextual analysis: for relevance, in order to understand the alignment with priorities and needs of key stakeholders; and for coherence, so as to understand linkages with other interventions. Relevance focuses on how an intervention responds to context. Coherence zooms out, looking at other interventions in that context and how they interact with the intervention being evaluated. Taken together, relevance and coherence can provide a clearer view of how the intervention affects – and is affected by – the context in which it is implemented.

- The analysis of relevance also relates to the impact criterion, which looks at the ultimate significance of an intervention – including its value to those affected. Evaluators should spend sufficient time examining the needs, priorities and policies of all actors (including potential tensions among them) to be able to sufficiently assess the overall relevance of the intervention and to further analyse its significance when looking at impact.

- Many of the elements of relevance are critical factors in efficiency and sustainability: a relevant intervention is likely to have greater support among stakeholders, which can influence the timeliness of delivery and use of resources, as well as the degree of ownership of the resulting benefits (and thus their sustainability).

Integrating inclusion

Understanding gendered power dynamics and reflecting on the SDG commitment to "leave no one behind" are crucial in understanding relevance. Gendered power dynamics and the marginalisation of certain groups – including racial/ethnic groups – are central considerations for understanding relevance in a particular context.

Understanding who was involved in intervention design and how they were involved, with special attention to power dynamics and marginalised groups, will help evaluators understand the relevance of the intervention as designed, as well as the extent to which the intervention was responsive to changing needs over time.

The definition of relevance above emphasises the importance of considering trade-offs between different needs and priorities, including greater consideration of equity and power dynamics between people affected by the intervention directly or indirectly.

Here there is a strong link with human rights and equality, particularly when an intersectional lens, which considers how multiple forms of social and political identity such as gender, disability, ethnicity, sexuality and social class combine to create discrimination and inequality, is applied. When identifying priorities for the analysis of relevance, it is essential to consider under-represented and marginalised groups (groups that may be restricted in their access to services and/or rights) and how their needs and priorities are – or are not – captured in formal documents and policies. In addition, it will be important to take into account whether the intervention incorporates different levels of access, given constraints faced by particular groups.

Challenges of evaluating relevance and how to address them

The table below identifies several common challenges when evaluating relevance – the range of needs and priorities to consider, poorly articulated objectives and changes in the context – and suggests ways of addressing them for both evaluators and evaluation managers.

Table 4.1. Challenges of evaluating relevance

Challenge	How to address: Evaluators	How to address: Evaluation managers
There are many national and international stakeholders to consider who have multiple and potentially competing priorities and needs.	A strong analysis of relevance should consider potential and actual trade-offs in responses to needs. The relevance of beneficiaries should be the most important consideration when looking at needs and priorities. Ownership and participation are also helpful for managing this challenge and in ensuring that competing priorities are accounted for and, where possible, balanced.	Clearly and succinctly define the beneficiaries of the intervention. If the results chain is very long, focus on the direct beneficiaries for the analysis of relevance and leave questions about ultimate beneficiaries to be analysed under effectiveness and impact.\n\nWhen narrowing the scope to decide whose needs and priorities are most important, consider the purpose of the evaluation and which component of relevance is most useful in supporting this. Careful consideration should be given to the evaluation's utility at the point of design.
Understanding if an intervention has clear and appropriate objectives and how they were determined.	To make a strong assessment of relevance, an intervention's objectives are a critical starting point. This can be a challenge if they are not clearly articulated. Evaluators should critically review the extent to which objectives are sufficiently challenging, reflect the needs of both the intended beneficiaries and the capacities of stakeholders, and explore how these objectives were identified and verified. The suitability of objectives might be further explored under impact to understand whether the objectives contributed to important, transformational changes.\n\nIn this instance, evaluators should engage closely with programme stakeholders to understand the programme's objectives, how they were defined and ascertain whether a contingency plan is/was in place. They should assess whether and to what extent these are based on a sound analysis of needs and context. This will form an important starting point for understanding relevance.	Evaluation managers should seek to establish the intervention's objectives as part of developing the terms of reference.\n\nThe terms of reference should enable evaluators to critically reflect on the extent to which objectives were appropriate to needs, external context and reflect feedback from stakeholders.
The intervention lacks a clearly articulated theory of change, logic model and/or other explicit design rationale.	Assessment of relevance is aided by a theory of change, logic model and/or other explicit design rationale as this provides important insights for assessing relevance of design. Evaluators should identify if this exists and, where necessary, work with stakeholders to help them reconstruct or clearly articulate the theory of change as a starting point for the evaluation.	Evaluation managers should seek to provide the programme/intervention's theory of change, logic model and/or other explicit design rationale documentation to evaluators at the outset of the evaluation.
The context changed over time, but it is unclear if – and how – the intervention was adapted.	Unfortunately adaptations are not always well documented. It is necessary to first describe	Evaluation managers can help identify and contact key decision makers who can help in

what changes occurred, and how the intervention was (or was not) adapted, in order to then evaluate relevance.	"reconstructing" the story of any adjustments made to the intervention. If decisions were not well documented, interviews can be useful in understanding what happened.
If it is clear that the context has changed significantly in ways that might have affected relevance, the evaluators should consult intervention documents (such as annual or quarterly reports, monitoring data, and, if possible, communications such as meeting minutes, announcements to staff and participants) to "reconstruct" the changes that were made, and identify key decision points and what drove those decisions.	

Examples of evaluating relevance

This section includes a cross section of examples from evaluating the relevance of general budget support, farmer livelihood supports and health sector programmes.

Box 4.1. Evaluating the relevance of general budget support

The OECD DAC EvalNet's methodological guidance for evaluating budget support suggests focusing on the relevance and appropriateness of the design of the budget support and the mix of inputs in relation to the political, economic and social context of the partner country, the government's policy framework, and the development partners' development assistance strategies.

An example of a key question for relevance is: To what extent was the design of the budget support programme appropriate and relevant given the political, economic and social context in the country, the government's policy framework and the external development partners' development assistance strategies?

For example, the evaluation of budget support in Tunisia (cited in the guidance) examined the extent to which the budget support used the right mix of technical assistance, policy dialogue and funds appropriate for the institutional context of the government of Tunisia and its priorities. In a first step, the evaluation looked at outcomes for the government (as a beneficiary). Outcomes for final beneficiaries – service users (such as young people attending tertiary education) – were included in a second step, which analysed effectiveness and impact.

Source: OECD (2011[3]), *Evaluating Budget Support: Methodological Approach*, https://www.oecd.org/dac/evaluation/dcdndep/Methodological%20approach%20BS%20evaluations%20Sept%202012%20_with%20cover%20Thi.pdf

---

Box 4.2. Evaluation of the "Improving Farmer Livelihoods" project in the Myanmar Dry Zone

This intervention and its evaluation focused on livelihoods and food security of communities of the poor and vulnerable in Myanmar's Central Dry Zone and provides a good example of how to apply the criterion of relevance in a tailored and appropriate way.

The assessment of relevance included considering the intervention's responsiveness to needs and priorities of stakeholders and how stakeholder groups were engaged throughout design and implementation.

The evaluation emphasised relevance over time, including the programme's adaptability to changing circumstances during implementation. In addition to relevance over the duration of the project, the evaluation also considered what relevance looked like at critical points, comparing the assessment of relevance from the mid-term review with current relevance at the time of the evaluation.

The evaluation found that the intervention was highly relevant to needs and context and particularly strong in adapting to environmental and policy changes over time. It applies relevance in an appropriate manner by employing and examining needs and context both at the design stage and during implementation to provide a well-rounded understanding of the intervention and its evolution.

Source: FAO (2020[4]), *Evaluation of "Improving farmer livelihoods in the dry zone through improved livestock health, productivity and marketing"*, http://www.fao.org/3/ca8463en/ca8463en.pdf

Box 4.3. Evaluating the relevance of health initiatives in Bolivia

This evaluation looked at health sector support from 2009-2020 in Bolivia. For relevance, the evaluation analysed not only the official approved requests of the Bolivian government, in particular the Ministry of Health, but also questioned the responsiveness to more specific needs of stakeholders, including beneficiaries. It concludes:

> *Relevance: The projects respond to the initiatives and requests of the institutions and authorities approved by the Ministry of Health, which means that Italian co-operation effectively responds to what the Bolivian government expresses as necessary. However, there is no proper process to identify the needs of the projects overall, which ends up generating problems of relevance and consistency. The most successful projects among those evaluated are those where at least an adequate knowledge of the specific needs to be met can be demonstrated.*

Source: Eurecna Spa (2020[5]), *Bolivia - Evaluation of health initiatives (2009-2020)*, http://www.oecd.org/derec/italy/evaluation-report-of-health-initiatives-in-Bolivia-2009_2020.pdf

Definition of coherence:

Coherence: How well does the intervention fit?

The compatibility of the intervention with other interventions in a country, sector or institution.

Note: The extent to which other interventions (particularly policies) support or undermine the intervention and vice versa. This includes internal coherence and external coherence. Internal coherence addresses the synergies and interlinkages between the intervention and other interventions carried out by the same institution/government, as well as the consistency of the intervention with the relevant international norms and standards to which that institution/government adheres. External coherence considers the consistency of the intervention with other actors' interventions in the same context. This includes complementarity, harmonisation and co-ordination with others, and the extent to which the intervention is adding value while avoiding duplication of effort.

What is coherence and why is it important?

In today's world, greater attention must be paid to coherence, with an increased focus on the synergies (or trade-offs) between policy areas and the growing attention to cross-government co-ordination. This is particularly the case in settings of conflict and humanitarian response, and when addressing the climate emergency.

In line with the 2030 Agenda and the SDGs, this new criterion encourages an integrated approach and provides an important lens for assessing coherence including synergies, cross-government co-ordination and alignment with international norms and standards. It is a place to consider different trade-offs and tensions, and to identify situations where duplication of efforts or inconsistencies in approaches to implementing policies across government or different institutions can undermine overall progress.

This criterion also encourages evaluators to understand the role of an intervention within a particular system (organisation, sector, thematic area, country), as opposed to taking an exclusively intervention- or institution-centric perspective. Whilst external coherence seeks to understand if and how closely policy objectives of actors are aligned with international development goals, it becomes incomplete if it does not consider the interests, influence and power of other external actors. As such, a wider political economy perspective is valuable to understanding the coherence of interventions.

In addition, the sources (both international and domestic) of financing for sustainable development are increasingly diverse. The reference to "international norms and standards" in the definition encourages analysis of the consistency of the intervention with the actor's own commitments under international law or agreements, such as anti-corruption statutes or human rights conventions. This applies to those agreements to which the entity has already committed and is therefore covered under internal coherence. Previously, this type of coherence was not often sufficiently analysed. International norms and standards may also be assessed under relevance from the viewpoint of responsiveness to global priorities, which is a complementary angle.

Understanding coherence: Elements for analysis

Coherence includes the dimensions of internal coherence and external coherence.

Internal coherence

Internal policy coherence considers two factors: the alignment with the wider policy frameworks of the institutions; and the alignment with other interventions implemented by the institution including those of other departments responsible for implementing development interventions or interventions which may affect the same operating context.[2] It should consider how harmonised these activities are, if duplication of effort and activities occurs, and if the interventions complement each other.

Within national governments (or, where applicable, other levels of government), challenges to coherence arise between different types of public policy, between different levels of government and between different stakeholders (both state and non-state, commercial and non-commercial). This should be carefully considered when evaluating coherence to understand where the intervention fits within this picture and the extent to which it is aligned with the policies governing the wider context.

For example, the Japanese Ministry of Foreign Affairs' ODA Evaluation Guidelines (Ministry of Foreign Affairs Japan, 2019[6]) support commissioners and implementers of evaluations in assessing the coherence of diplomatic and development strategies and actions across the Japanese Government. These guidelines provide a framework and advice to help evaluators consider interconnections, complementarity and coherence of diplomatic and official development assistance (ODA) strategies. This supports a holistic analysis of Japan's engagement and support for different sectors and countries.

Policy coherence can be understood from a horizontal perspective. For example, in the humanitarian-development-peace nexus there may be a strong need for coherence as one actor may have interventions covering development, military and security policy. In the environmental field, this could also refer to the need for coherence across the water-energy-food nexus, or the gender equality-climate change nexus. In other contexts, the ways in which non-development policy areas, such as trade, affect the intervention could be considered.

From a vertical perspective, policy coherence can be understood at different levels of an institution, or across different parts of a single government's development finance (e.g. its bilateral agency, development finance institute [DFI] and multilateral support). It could also consider how the intervention supports or undermines policy goals across geographic levels. For example, it can consider how well a local development intervention aligns with national development objectives and interventions at a national level or vice versa.

External coherence

External coherence has two main considerations: alignment with external policy commitments; and coherence with interventions implemented by other actors in a specific context.

From a policy perspective, external coherence considers the intervention's alignment with external policy commitments such as the SDGs, and how these are taken into account in the intervention's design and implementation. It is important to consider an institution's commitment to the SDGs at this point, as SDG Target 17.14 under Goal 17 aims to "enhance policy coherence for sustainable development". This is an important consideration as it encapsulates how both policy alignment and accountability for the SDGs are mainstreamed and implemented in practice.

Looking at implementation in specific context, evaluators should consider coherence with interventions implemented by other actors. For example, how are services provided by a range of actors – are there overlaps or gaps? Coherence considers how the intervention adds value in relation to others and how duplication of effort is avoided.

An evaluation of external coherence should maintain focus on the specific intervention or institution at hand while situating it within the wider context of humanitarian and sustainable development actors. This can include whether interventions are designed within and using existing systems and structures such as coordination mechanisms at the country or sector levels.

Connections with other criteria

Coherence is connected in particular with relevance, effectiveness and impact.

- While relevance assesses the intervention at the level of the needs and priorities of the stakeholders and beneficiaries that are directly involved, coherence goes up to the next level and looks at the fit of the intervention within the broader system. Both relevance and coherence consider how the intervention aligns with the context, but they do so from different perspectives.
- Coherence is often a useful angle through which to begin examining unintended effects, which can be captured under effectiveness and impact. While the intervention may achieve its objectives (effectiveness) these gains may be reversed by other (not coherent) interventions in the context.
- Likewise there are links with efficiency: incoherent interventions may be duplicative, thus wasting resources.

Integrating inclusion

Internal coherence provides a useful lens for considering inclusion, in particular as it relates to human rights commitments, norms and standards. Evaluators can consider the intervention's compatibility with inclusion and equality norms and standards at a national or institutional level for the implementing institutions and perspectives of local organisations, such as grassroots indigenous peoples' groups and disabled people's organisations. Assessment of coherence can provide useful insights into the value and coherence of activities that aim to reduce exclusion, reach marginalised and vulnerable groups, and transform gender inequalities.

Analysis of inclusion in relation to coherence should be considered when evaluators explore the extent to which impact was inclusive and the intervention was relevant, as there are synergies between these three areas of evaluative enquiry.

Challenges of evaluating coherence and how to address them

The table below identifies several of the key challenges when evaluating coherence – including challenges related to breadth of scope, mandate and data availability. Suggestions are made for ways of addressing them for both evaluators and evaluation managers.

Table 4.2. Challenges of evaluating coherence

Challenge	How to address: Evaluators	How to address: Evaluation managers
Policy coherence is challenging in many contexts/countries, as rigorous assessment requires access to a large volume of policy documents, data and informants.	Challenges can only be solved by applying qualitative assessments based on the available sources of data/information. It is also important to assess evaluability during the inception of an evaluation and be open and transparent about limitations. It should be flagged when data sources cannot be accessed. Understand the legislative environment and organisational policies and use knowledge to design appropriate primary data collection and analysis plans.	Evaluation managers should consider evaluability, data limitations and access when commissioning an evaluation. These should be anticipated to the greatest extent possible and discussed and mitigated with the evaluation team during inception.
Organisations restricting access to data due to data protection legislation and/or organisational policies.		Consider data limitations and access when designing and commissioning an evaluation. Ongoing discussions should be held with the evaluation team to support access to data and to develop suitable risk mitigation strategies.
Assessing coherence across all relevant policy areas can lead to a very broad scope.	Collaborate with the evaluation manager to ensure priorities and scope are clearly defined at the start of the evaluation.	Decide how coherence should be prioritised by defining scope and prioritising policy areas for consideration. This should be driven by the purpose and utilisation of the evaluation. When evaluating policy coherence in a particular sector, national institutions should co-ordinate as much as possible the evaluation of coherence within that sector.
The mandates of some evaluation departments may focus only on humanitarian and development assistance, limiting their scope to assess coherence questions across government.	Special attention should be paid at the evaluation design stage to define and refine the scope of the evaluation, and to operationalise how coherence would be explored in line with evaluation departments' mandates – or to outline limitations in doing so.	Coherence requires the recognition that policy areas beyond development may impact an evaluation. In theory, this gives evaluators greater liberty to explore areas beyond the intervention's immediate influence. However, there are challenges of operationalising it when looking across other policy areas that go beyond the institution's mandate. This is an evaluability consideration that should ideally be addressed before the evaluation. Institutions should determine whether to assess coherence in restricted areas. If this is a priority, evaluators or evaluation managers could negotiate with other departments to conduct a joint evaluation.

Examples of evaluating coherence

Though coherence is a new criterion for the OECD DAC, it has featured in many evaluations over the years. The criterion of coherence is also routinely used in humanitarian evaluations. This section includes a cross section of examples demonstrating how coherence has been evaluated in a strategic evaluation of policy coherence for development in Norway, natural disaster recovery in the Philippines and a country-portfolio evaluation in Montenegro.

Box 4.4. Evaluation of Norwegian efforts to ensure policy coherence for development

The Norwegian government has on several occasions committed to ensuring policy coherence for development in its interventions. Policy coherence is understood as "working on wider aspects of development in addition to development aid, such as trade, migration, investments, climate change and security". This evaluation considers policy "dilemmas" where there is a clear contradiction between the policy of different actors or policy areas. The report calls for "a more open and transparent discussion on real dilemmas and priorities, as there are some true dilemmas and choices to be made".

The purpose of the evaluation was to understand policy dilemmas and challenges of achieving policy coherence for development. It considers coherence within an individual country context and on a global scale. Both the internal and external elements of coherence are explored:

- internal policy coherence of interventions led by the Ministry of Foreign Affairs and other Norwegian actors
- external coherence to understand how aligned the actors' policy objectives were with international development objectives.

Using Myanmar as a case study, the evaluation considers policy inconsistencies between development policy and other policy areas. Myanmar was selected because of the diverse range of traditional and non-traditional Norwegian development actors involved in the country and the potential conflicts that arise between their policy priorities on a local level. The evaluation takes an interesting methodological approach to understanding policy dilemmas. It examines where challenges have been raised by non-governmental organisations (NGOs), political organisations or international institutions, signalling incoherent policy across Norwegian priorities and interventions. For example, it raised two dilemmas: Norway's business engagement in Myanmar and its commitment to peacebuilding; and the engagement in national resource development and the commitment to peace. This analysis also highlights a major challenge in both evaluating and acting on coherence. Indeed, the Ministry is not mandated to intervene with regard to other ministries' policy decisions, thus complicating its ability to understand and resolve inconsistencies. Looking to the global scale, the evaluation also considered external incoherence with Norway's global commitments. It found challenges of aligning domestic policy with international development priorities.

The evaluation shows a thoughtful application of coherence by illustrating the challenges of implementing policy-coherent interventions that are sensitive to both the operational context and institutional priorities.

Source: Norad (2018[7]), *Evaluation of Norwegian Efforts to Ensure Policy Coherence for Development*, https://www.norad.no/contentassets/4ac3de36fbdd4229811a423f4b00acf7/8.18-evaluation-of-norwegian-efforts-to-ensure-policy-coherence-for-development.pdf

Box 4.5. Evaluating the coherence of natural disaster reconstruction assistance in the Philippines

This evaluation considers Canada's international assistance programming and role as a donor with regard to natural disasters. It illustrates how coherence can be considered both externally and internally for an intervention. It considers the CAD 20.5 million Haiyan reconstruction programme and the bilateral relationship between Canada and the Philippines from 2013-14 to 2018-19.

Evaluation of coherence

Although it was conducted before coherence was incorporated as an OECD DAC evaluation criterion, the evaluation clearly focuses on coherence, even if this is not explicitly stated. The evaluation considers coherence in relation to both the external and internal elements of analysis.

- External coherence – the evaluation examines Canada's role as a donor, its behaviour across operational and political contexts, and how this intervention fit into those contexts. The evaluation highlighted an alignment with the Philippine government's priorities and national recovery programme and considered complementarity with other programmes operating in the region.

- Internal coherence – the evaluation examined Canada's international assistance programming and contextualised this within a wider sample of international assistance programming. It placed a particular emphasis on the programme's alignment with Canada's broader policy and assessed the extent to which the intervention was typical of Canada's approach in disaster relief responses.

It also shows how closely coherence and relevance intersect as the intervention is continuously related back to stakeholder and contextual needs and priorities – both elements for analysis of relevance. However, the evaluation takes this a step further, to understand not just the responsiveness of the intervention but also alignment and consideration in designing and implementing a clear, policy-coherent intervention that matched Canada's wider interest in the Philippines and was consistent with their other disaster relief programmes.

Source: Global Affairs Canada (2019[8]), *Evaluation of Natural Disaster Reconstruction Assistance in the Philippines, 2013-14 to 2018-19*, https://www.international.gc.ca/gac-amc/publications/evaluation/2019/endra-earcn-philippines.aspx?lang=eng

---

Box 4.6. Evaluating the coherence of Slovenia's development co-operation with Montenegro

This evaluation describes the implementation of development co-operation between the Republic of Slovenia and Montenegro from 2013-2016. The evaluation aimed "to provide evidence of performance (i.e. to what extent does it achieve the objectives of development co-operation), to analyse the reasons for success and failure in performance, and to provide recommendations for formulating policies, programmes and projects in the future."

The evaluation included coherence as one of eight criteria (programme management, delivery, and added value for Slovenia were also included), asking the following question:

- Have contradictions with other policies prevented the implementation and achievement of the development objectives, or are policies mutually reinforcing?

The evaluation looked at external coherence with other policies related to development co-operation including the EU negotiation process and investments in environmental infrastructure. The evaluation concluded that the programmes were aligned with other policies.

The evaluation also looked at complementarity with other donor activities and found that the lack of sufficient donor co-ordination systems in Montenegro hindered the achievement of complementarity or the prevention of duplication.

Source: Slovenia's Ministry of Foreign Affairs (2017[9]), *Evaluation of Slovenia's Development Cooperation with Montenegro 2013-2016 period: Final Report*, https://www.gov.si/assets/ministrstva/MZZ/Dokumenti/multilaterala/razvojno-sodelovanje/Development-cooperation-with-Montenegro-evaluation-final-report.pdf

Effectiveness

Definition of effectiveness:

Effectiveness: Is the intervention achieving its objectives?

The extent to which the intervention achieved, or is expected to achieve, its objectives and its results, including any differential results across groups.

Note: Analysis of effectiveness involves taking account of the relative importance of the objectives or results. The term effectiveness is also used as an aggregate measure of the extent to which an intervention has achieved or is expected to achieve relevant and sustainable impacts, efficiently and coherently.

What is effectiveness and why is it important?

Effectiveness helps in understanding the extent to which an intervention is achieving or has achieved its objectives. It can provide insight into whether an intervention has attained its planned results, the process by which this was done, which factors were decisive in this process and whether there were any unintended effects. Effectiveness is concerned with the most closely attributable results and it is important to differentiate it from impact, which examines higher-level effects and broader changes.

Examining the achievement of objectives on the results chain or causal pathway requires a clear understanding of the intervention's aims and objectives. Therefore, using the effectiveness lens can assist evaluators, programme managers or officers and others in developing (or evaluating) clear objectives. Likewise, effectiveness can be useful for evaluators in identifying whether achievement of results (or lack thereof) is due to shortcomings in the intervention's implementation or its design.

Under the effectiveness criterion, evaluators should also identify unintended effects. Ideally, project managers will have identified risks during the design phase and evaluators can make use of this analysis as they begin their assessment. An exploration of unintended effects is important both for identifying negative results (e.g. an exacerbation of conflict dynamics) or positive ones (e.g. innovations that improve effectiveness). Institutions commissioning evaluations may want to provide evaluators with guidance on minimum standards for identifying unintended effects, particularly where these involve human rights violations or other grave unintended consequences.

The definition of effectiveness encourages evaluators and managers to ask important questions about the distribution of results across different groups, whether intended or not. This is deliberate and intended to strengthen considerations of equity, which is in line with the SDG policy priority to "leave no one behind". It encourages evaluators to examine equity issues, whether or not equity is a specific objective of the intervention. Such analysis requires data and may entail an investment of resources – which is often justified because of the valuable insights the evaluation can provide.[3]

In drawing conclusions about effectiveness, evaluations should concentrate on the results that are most important in the context and for the evaluation audience. The term "relative importance" emphasises the message that one should exercise evaluative judgement and weigh the importance of the achieved/unachieved objectives and results, including unintended consequences, when drawing conclusions about effectiveness.

Understanding effectiveness: Elements for analysis

The definition of effectiveness includes the key concepts of: achievement of objectives, the varying importance of objectives and results, differential results across groups and understanding the factors that influence outcomes.

Achievement of the objectives

The primary focus of assessing effectiveness remains on establishing whether an intervention has achieved its intended results at different levels of the results chain (usually outputs and outcomes but also in some cases impacts). The results chain should be specified as part of the design of the intervention and is the key reference point for management, monitoring and evaluation.

It is very difficult to assess the effectiveness of an activity if the stated objectives or planned results of the activity are vague or ambiguous or have shifted during the course of the intervention without it being updated or restructured. Intervention managers should at least explain why goals have changed and what the new goals are. If this has not been done, evaluators will need to consult intervention documents or interview stakeholders to recreate the logic underpinning changes in the intervention over time. Based on the reconstructed logic, evaluators can then judge the extent to which the new objectives were relevant and effectively reached.

Evaluating effectiveness is also important in adaptive programmes where changes are made iteratively, based on feedback from stakeholders, emerging results and changes in context. In adaptive programmes, the design and implementation of an intervention may go through numerous incremental changes over time. In these situations, it is important for evaluators to reflect on and review theories of change with reference to wider systems in which an intervention is located and take into account any records showing how and why changes have been made. The evaluation of effectiveness should reflect current objectives. Reviewing the logic and need for changes to implementation or objectives (often captured in updated theories of change or results frameworks) should inform evaluations of effectiveness.

Evaluating effectiveness may involve establishing observable changes in the target group or environment over the intervention's implementation as well as establishing causality of the observed changes at different levels, i.e. showing that the changes were caused by the intervention or that the intervention contributed to the changes as opposed to other environmental factors or, alternatively, another intervention. Methodologies should be designed to allow the evaluator to draw out how results came about and what the reasons (explanatory factors) were for achievement, underachievement or non-achievement.

Evaluating effectiveness includes examining the intervention's results. Results is defined by the OECD DAC as the intervention's output, outcome or impact (intended or unintended, positive and/or negative) (OECD, 2002[10]). Therefore evaluating effectiveness may also include the assessment of any unintended effects, both positive and negative that have occurred as a result of the intervention. The implementation of interventions always has the potential to cause unintended social, economic or environmental effects, or may cause effects that are not intended but could have been foreseen. Therefore, evaluations should be careful to consider effects that fall outside of those specified in the intervention objectives. This can also extend to examining the potential benefits or risks arising from these unintended (predictable or unpredictable) effects. The extent to which the intervention contributed to the realisation of national or other relevant development goals and objectives in the context also falls under effectiveness – while the potential for these contributions will be examined under relevance.

Weighing the relative importance of what was achieved

When evaluating effectiveness, evaluators explore the achievement (or lack of achievement) of the various objectives and results of the intervention. If some – but not all – of the objectives were achieved the evaluators will need to examine their relative importance to draw conclusions on the effectiveness. This may draw on the analysis of relevance, which should have addressed the potential differences between the priorities and needs of the various stakeholders. This implies that evaluators may conclude the intervention was effective in some ways but not others, or effective from the perspective of some stakeholders, but not others.

Differential results

Evaluators should consider inclusiveness and equity of results amongst beneficiary groups – whether the beneficiaries are individuals or institutions. Understanding differential results can include looking at the extent to which the intervention ensured an inclusive approach in design and implementation. For example, an evaluation could examine the process through which the intervention's objectives were formulated. This includes whether the objectives were formulated based on a needs analysis and consultation process amongst stakeholders (including the main target group). Through this process, insight may also be gained into whether the intervention missed any opportunities to generate results for its target population or beneficiaries, including contributing to longer term change, such as reduction in inequalities. Evaluators may examine unintended or unexpected results as well as the intended result, taking into account the fact that certain changes and transformations are subtle and/or long term and may be difficult to quantify.

Influencing factors

Examining the factors that influence results is important because it helps evaluators to understand *why* an intervention may or may not have achieved its goals, which helps partners identify areas for improvement. Factors may be internal to the intervention or external. Such factors might include those related to: management, human resources, financial aspects, regulatory aspects, implementation modifications or deviation from plans. Quality of implementation (and adherence to implementation protocols) is often a driving factor of effectiveness, and should be described before evaluating effectiveness, efficiency, impact and sustainability.

Externally, evaluators should consider positive and negative effects arising from the intervention's context, which in turn contribute to achievement or non-achievement of results. This can include assessing the intervention's adaptive capacity in response to contextual changes. Evaluations can also examine the timeliness of results (e.g. phasing of support to target groups or environments which aided delivery of results).

Connections with other criteria

Effectiveness is linked with other criteria, particularly relevance and impact:

- Under relevance, the objectives of the intervention are identified; progress towards these objectives is determined by effectiveness. It is of course possible that an intervention that is not relevant, is nonetheless delivered effectively. In the case of such a disconnect, evaluators will need to use judgement when drawing conclusions overall, as one cannot simply ignore findings from one criterion in favour of another.
- Effectiveness and impact are complementary criteria focusing on different levels of the results chain. Effectiveness considers the achievement of results relative to an intervention's objectives, namely at the output and outcome level whereas impact focuses on higher-level results, namely what the declared higher-level results are and what contributes to these. In general, intervention managers and evaluations should ensure that a clear distinction is made between the different results levels (i.e. input, output, outcome and impact) and that it is clear which aspects will be evaluated under each criterion.

Integrating inclusion

The definition of effectiveness encourages an in-depth consideration of equity between different groups. Evaluators should assess how inclusive the intervention has been for different beneficiary groups and how key principles such as equity, non-discrimination and accountability have been incorporated at all stages, from design through to results. In accordance with "leave no one behind" particular attention should be given to the extent to which the intervention has met the needs of the most marginalised. It is important to examine the achievement and distribution of results in relation to various beneficiary groups and explain any differences.

Moreover, evaluators should consider if, how and why results contribute to tackling inequality. Under this criterion evaluators should examine how specific activities impact the welfare of specific groups and whether these activities provide participants with opportunities for empowerment.

Challenges of evaluating effectiveness and how to address them

The table below identifies challenges related to data, formulation of objectives and attribution of results, and suggests ways of addressing them for both evaluators and evaluation managers.

Table 4.3. Challenges of evaluating effectiveness

Challenge	How to address: Evaluators	How to address: Evaluation managers
Lack of appropriate, informative or disaggregated data.	The availability of data (e.g. a lack of baseline or mid-term assessments) can inhibit the measurement of the achievement of objectives as causality is then more difficult to attribute and it is harder to determine who is contributing what. Baseline data can be reconstructed but this is generally less precise and reliable than properly assembled baseline data. Other approaches evaluators can take include: 1) triangulation and validation of data that is available; 2) use of alternative methods; and 3) the construction of a contribution story.	Ideally, data availability should be planned for during intervention design to ensure that appropriate, informative and disaggregated data is collected throughout the lifespan of the intervention. Evaluation managers should have a clear picture of available data, possible alternative sources and work with the evaluators to develop alternative approaches where data is not available. Collect diagnostics from other evaluations and research reports in the area. Review and consider how to apply or learn from previous work on the development of indicators in related areas of work, including SDG targets.
Working with poorly phrased, vague or difficult-to-measure objectives/purpose statements.	Ensure that intervention objectives are verifiable, realistic and aligned with current international standards for development interventions in the inception phase of an evaluation. The indicators for measuring the achievement of the objectives should also be validated according to generally accepted criteria such as SMART (Specific, Measurable, Attainable, Realistic and Timely). Ideally, this process should be undertaken in a participatory manner between the evaluators and evaluation managers.	Work in conjunction with evaluators to identify clear criteria for measuring the achievement of objectives in accordance with generally accepted standards (e.g. SMART indicators). For gender-sensitive evaluations, consider moving from SMART and RACER indicators to CREAM (clear, relevant, economic, adequate and monitorable) and SPICED (subjective, participatory, interpreted, cross-checked and compared, empowering, diverse and disaggregated) indicators. Improve the definition and concreteness of goals and results, within the framework of the programme theory/theory of change defined at the time. When there is no theory of change, try to rebuild a valid one to contextualise the internal logic of the intervention. Improve the coherence of the formulation, a posteriori, by relocating the project on the basis of participatory practices and with the involvement of the stakeholders.
Attribution of results	The issue of attributing causality or determining contribution is a challenge in evaluating effectiveness, particularly over the longer term. The construction of a contribution story and devising appropriate triangulation of data streams can support the evaluator to identify whether results can be attributed to the intervention being evaluated.	Opinions, evaluations and judgements of stakeholders who are knowledgeable about the intervention/entity and who might be possible partners in implementing the intervention or in achieving development results are taken into account.

Examples of evaluating effectiveness

This section includes a cross section of examples demonstrating how effectiveness has been evaluated in regards to electoral assistance and a country programme evaluation in Cabo Verde.

Box 4.7. Evaluation of the effectiveness and inclusiveness of Australian electoral assistance

From the 1970s onwards, Australia has provided electoral assistance to a range of developing countries with the aim of supporting them in their transition to and consolidation of formal, deeply rooted and functioning democracies. This evaluation examined Australia's assistance to national elections in eight countries in the Asia-Pacific region from 2006-16. It provides a good example of applying the criterion of effectiveness with particular reference to changing objectives over time and also considering effectiveness in relation to inclusion, gender and vulnerable groups.

The evaluation considered the overall objectives of Australian electoral assistance and then focused on effectiveness and inclusion across three key areas: strengthening electoral management systems, promoting participation and supporting the organisation of elections.

The evaluation also noted that Australia's objectives related to electoral assistance shifted within the implementation period and the evaluation thus accounts for this shift in objectives in their analysis. In addition, the evaluation also closely examines the risks associated with providing effective and inclusive electoral assistance, accounting for the external factors that may inhibit the effectiveness of the current and future interventions.

In considering the objectives, the evaluation focused specifically on the inclusiveness of the results, which is useful in illustrating how evaluations can examine differential results across groups of people when assessing effectiveness. The achievement of results was examined through a gender lens with the evaluation utilising qualitative findings to reveal that social norms and legal and institutional barriers were leading to disproportionately lower numbers of voter participation amongst women.

The evaluation also accounted for the inclusion of vulnerable groups, namely disability inclusion, finding that equity in results between different groups was also limited due to cultural barriers despite activities to improve physical access. From these findings, the evaluation was able to make recommendations for future interventions that focused on increasing the equity of results, which in turn supports the wider achievement of intervention results and development goals.

Source: Arghiros et al. (2017[11]), *Making it Count: Lessons from Australian Electoral Assistance 2006-16,* http://www.oecd.org/derec/australia/australia-electoral-assistance-2006-2016.pdf

---

Box 4.8. Evaluating the effectiveness of the African Development Bank's country strategy and programme in Cabo Verde

This evaluation of the African Development Bank's (AfDB) support in the electricity sector in Cabo Verde provides an example of how the effectiveness criterion is applied in practice, including considering relevance of design and implementation, with particular attention to gender and social inclusion objectives. The AfDB had several broad objectives for its assistance, which included helping the country foster inclusive growth through infrastructure development and good governance reforms and the strategic aim of helping the country transition towards "green growth" or low-emissions, climate-resilient development.

In order to assess the effectiveness of the intervention and whether these objectives had been met, the evaluation assessed whether the intervention had achieved the following planned development outcomes:

- increased access to electricity supply for the population
- increase in the proportion of renewable energy
- increased availability of arable land and water supply
- improvements in good governance.

In doing so, the evaluation also analysed internal factors such as the robustness of design and the progress of implementation, as well as external factors affecting the intervention. Special attention was also paid to gender equality and social inclusion when addressing equity of results.

It found that while solid progress was registered in helping the country foster inclusive growth through infrastructure development and good governance reforms, the strategic aim of helping the country transition towards "green growth" or low-emission, climate-resilient development was ill-matched with available resources and instruments. The evaluation found that examining effectiveness can shed light on whether the planned results of an intervention have been achieved, as well as on the factors that influenced the delivery of results.

Source: IDEV (2018[12]), *Cabo Verde: Evaluation of the Bank's Country Strategy and Program 2008–2017: Summary Report*, http://www.oecd.org/derec/afdb/AfDB-2008-2017-cabo-verde-bank-strategy.pdf

Definition of efficiency:

Efficiency: How well are resources being used?

The extent to which the intervention delivers, or is likely to deliver, results in an economic and timely way.

Note: "Economic" is the conversion of inputs (funds, expertise, natural resources, time, etc.) into outputs, outcomes and impacts, in the most cost-effective way possible, as compared to feasible alternatives in the context. "Timely" delivery is within the intended timeframe, or a timeframe reasonably adjusted to the demands of the evolving context. This may include assessing operational efficiency (how well the intervention was managed).

What is efficiency and why is it important?

This criterion is an opportunity to check whether an intervention's resources can be justified by its results, which is of major practical and political importance. Efficiency matters to many stakeholder groups, including governments, civil society and beneficiaries. Better use of limited resources means that more can be achieved with development co-operation, for example in progressing towards the SDGs where the needs are huge. Efficiency is of particular interest to governments that are accountable to their taxpayers, who often question the value for money of different policies and programmes, particularly decisions on international development co-operation, which tends to be more closely scrutinised.

Operationally, efficiency is also important. Many interventions encounter problems with feasibility and implementation, particularly with regard to the way in which resources are used. Evaluation of efficiency helps to improve managerial incentives to ensure programmes are well conducted, holding managers to account for how they have taken decisions and managed risks.

There are several important assumptions and points to note:

- Resources should be understood in the broadest sense and include full economic costs (human, environmental, financial and time). It is not the same as the programme budget or the money spent.
- Results should also be understood in a comprehensive sense, covering the whole of the results chain: outputs, outcomes and impacts. Depending on the type of evaluation, some organisations associate efficiency with outputs only; however, the criteria is defined and conceptualised here to encourage evaluating efficiency also in relation to higher-level effects such as impacts, though this can often be challenging.
- Evaluability: The ability to assess effectiveness, impact, coherence and sustainability affects what can be said about efficiency.
- Efficiency is about choices between feasible alternatives that can deliver similar results within the given resources. Before cost-effectiveness comparisons can be made, alternatives must be identified that are genuinely feasible and comparable in terms of quality and results.

For these reasons, efficiency analysis should be firmly grounded in analysis of the context, since for a given example it may be more costly to reach the intended beneficiaries but also more important and justifiable in terms of development impacts.

Understanding efficiency: Elements for analysis

Evaluating efficiency involves looking at the key areas of economic efficiency, operational efficiency, and timeliness.

Economic efficiency

This is the primary element for analysing efficiency. Economic efficiency is used here to refer to the absence of waste and the conversion of inputs into results in the most cost-efficient way possible. It includes assessing the efficiency of results at all levels of the results chain: outputs, outcomes and impacts. This also involves evaluating the extent to which appropriate choices were made and trade-offs addressed in the design stage and during implementation. These choices include the way that resources were allocated between target groups and time periods, as well as the options that were available for purchasing inputs according to market conditions.

Operational efficiency

Operational efficiency is also an important element to consider. It deals with how well resources are used during implementation. Questions to help explore operational efficiency include: Were the human and financial resources used as planned and appropriately and fully utilised (or were resources misallocated, budgets underspent, overspent)? Were resources redirected as needs changed? Were risks managed? Were decisions taken which helped to enhance efficiency in response to new information? Were the logistics and procurement decisions optimal?

Timeliness

Closely related to both economic and operational efficiency, timeliness starts by asking whether and to what extent the results were achieved within the intended timeframe. It is also the opportunity to check if the timeframe was realistic or appropriate in the first place. In addition, was it reasonably adjusted during the intervention, given that for many interventions external factors and changes to the programme are likely? Evaluators must assess if efforts were made to overcome obstacles and mitigate delays in how the intervention was managed, as the situation evolved.

Connections with other criteria

As already noted, the different criteria are connected and should be seen as alternative lenses for looking at the intervention, rather than rigid boundaries. Some of the interconnections with other criteria are:

- Relevance and efficiency: A key aspect of operational relevance is whether the intervention design responded well to the context allowing for considerations of feasibility and capacity. In practical terms, whether the design was feasible and could be implemented also has a direct effect on efficiency. Thus, in this specific aspect the evaluator may end up looking at both issues together.
- Efficiency and results: Since efficiency involves assessing to what extent the resources used were converted into results, all aspects of results (i.e. questions arising when assessing effectiveness, impact and sustainability) should be considered. Operational efficiency is closely related to effectiveness and impact. Often, looking at how well things are working within an intervention involves looking at effectiveness and efficiency simultaneously. This is particularly true, for instance, when identifying bottlenecks and how to address them, or ensuring resources are allocated to where they are needed.

Integrating inclusion

Through the lens of the efficiency criterion, evaluators can understand how inclusion is integrated and understood in the intervention's management and the extent to which resource use reflects differential experiences and results for different people. The cost of achieving results often varies across beneficiaries, with those "furthest behind" being the most difficult – and expensive – to reach. Analysis of efficiency should therefore be infused with a clear understanding of inequalities and power dynamics in the context, as well as an understanding of how the intervention fits with the need for transformational change to address underlying inequalities. Efficiency analysis is a key place to consider whether or not a commitment to the "leave no one behind" agenda (and the 2030 Agenda aim of achieving transformational change for marginalised groups) has been meaningfully and effectively operationalised across management, decision making and resource allocation.

Here, analysis can include how and why resources are allocated between the different groups being targeted by an intervention and the extent to which resource allocation was based on needs and engagement with marginalised groups. Evaluators can consider if inclusive and equitable results are achieved at a reasonable cost, how "reasonable cost" is defined and determined and how such a cost varies between different groups of beneficiaries. For instance, if the intervention commits to reaching specific groups, are sufficient resources allocated and justified so as to do this successfully?

Understanding whose voices are heard and listened to when decisions are made about how policies are designed, how funds are spent and who has control and oversight of these processes is a key consideration. When intervention logic and plans include changing unequal structures and power dynamics, evaluations should consider the extent to which they have been successful or whether they have unintentionally reinforced existing unequal structures and dynamics.

It is also important to consider whether interventions collect relevant, disaggregated monitoring data to enable implementers to take relevant decisions on the focus of activities/objectives and resources allocated to inclusive development.

Challenges of evaluating efficiency and how to address them

The appropriate way of applying the efficiency criterion will depend entirely on the nature of the intervention itself and will be different for projects, programmes, country programmes and policies. The following example from the Dutch Ministry of Foreign Affairs shows an application of the criterion at the policy level within the water sector, where efficiency is understood largely in terms of co-ordination and practical aspects of planning and partnerships across a complex set of relationships (Box 4.11).

Table 4.4 identifies several of the key challenges when evaluating efficiency and suggests ways of addressing them for both evaluators and evaluation managers.

A basic decision is whether and how to use traditional economic measures and related tools such as cost-benefit analysis, rates of return, cost-effectiveness analysis, benchmarking comparisons, etc. to evaluate efficiency.[4] This depends on the purpose of the evaluation, the intervention and intended results, feasibility, available data/resources, and the intended audience.

The usefulness of different analytical tools will also depend on what approach was used at the design/approval stages within the relevant institution, as this will have major implications for the availability of information required to undertake different types of analysis. Within multilateral development banks and in some public sector capital investment programmes, very clear guidance is provided on economic, social and environmental appraisal *ex ante* and increasingly on applying gender analysis to such projects and programmes. It makes sense to use the same tools for assessing efficiency during project appraisal or approval (generally *ex ante*, before the intervention is implemented) as those used during evaluation. The policy rules and guidance adopted by the institution will also partly determine what data and indicators are available to the evaluator (e.g. whether rates of return were estimated during the economic appraisal, if one exists, and whether alternatives were identified).

Table 4.4. Challenges of evaluating efficiency

Challenge	How to address: Evaluators	How to address: Evaluation managers
Finding suitable comparisons	Evaluators usually struggle to find perfect matches, so they use what is available. Yet, they must be cautious in making comparisons and should undertake a sensitivity analysis. For example, efficiency in fragile and conflict-affected situations should only be compared with similarly challenging environments.	Where evaluation managers have access to data or analyses that could provide useful background information for evaluators, plan to incorporate these resources in the documentation provided to evaluators.
Navigating different concepts of efficiency and the associated methods and tools	The literature on the economic concepts of efficiency is extensive and can be consulted by evaluators to decide on which methods and tools are most appropriate given the evaluation at hand. The BMZ working paper provides an excellent summary of these (Palenberg, 2011[13]).	
Lack of adequate expertise on efficiency analysis	Ensure there is an understanding on what is needed to conduct an efficiency analysis and how to incorporate it into the evaluation process (both in terms of approach and expertise).	Ensure that the terms of reference for evaluations specify the required efficiency analysis expertise.
Data and measurement	Available data on benefits, results and costs can be hard to obtain. For example, impact evaluations may provide quantified estimates of changes in outcomes due to the intervention while, generally speaking, leaving out estimates of costs, let alone full costs.	Ensure that evaluators have access to the necessary data for efficiency analysis (e.g. data on the cost/benefit of a given intervention or action, in terms of budget, human resources, time, etc.).
Time considerations	Both in economic appraisal and in evaluation of efficiency, choices between time periods when resources are used and when results are delivered are a crucial aspect. Results and full costs (e.g. environmental costs) may accrue over many years, so the actual efficiency during the course of the programme, or at the time of the evaluation, may not reflect the entire picture.	Efficiency is affected by a series of choices during the programme or intervention including how managers responded to shifts in priorities, anticipated or reacted to risks, dealt with cost overruns, and so forth.

Examples of evaluating efficiency

This section includes a cross section of examples demonstrating how efficiency has been evaluated in cases of rural electrification, agricultural input subsidies and a significant portfolio of work on water management.

Box 4.9. Evaluating the efficiency of the World Bank's support of rural electrification

This study focused on the World Bank's programme of lending support to rural electrification in a range of countries between 1980 and 2006, including a portfolio review covering 120 projects, 10 country case studies and analysis of existing survey data (energy and household surveys for 12 countries).

Drawing on the rich datasets available in a large multilateral development bank with a long history of working in this sector, it considered efficiency from various angles, including comparing costs and benefits. The portfolio review draws on estimates of rates of return for projects in the bank's portfolio, since these are routinely included in validated completion reports for infrastructure projects. Going beyond this, the welfare impacts are estimated using consumer surplus estimates, which enable evaluators to assess the interventions' benefits and related costs. The evaluation shows one approach to assessing impact, elements of equity (reaching the poor) and understanding the trade-offs between sustainability, economic and allocative efficiency, overall impact and impact by target groups.

Source: IEG (2008[14]), *The Welfare Impact of Rural Electrification: A Reassessment of the Costs and Benefits*, https://openknowledge.worldbank.org/handle/10986/6519

Box 4.10. Evaluating the efficiency of agricultural input subsidies in Sub-Saharan Africa

This study evaluated agricultural input subsidies in Ghana, Malawi, Tanzania and Zambia, including so-called "smart subsidies" which are specifically designed to maximise effects at the lowest cost.

Evaluation of efficiency

Because of the nature of the topic, economic efficiency – here used in the sense of whether the subsidies are worth their cost in various respects – is a central issue in this study.
The study draws on estimates of changes in agricultural productivity and then discusses whether these are proportionate to the costs, providing a reasonable return and what factors, such as targeting, played a role. For example, in relation to Zambia the study notes that:

> *Greater use of agricultural input appears to have substantial effects on maize production, but the extra output comes at a very high cost. The best estimates available suggest that it would be cheaper to import maize for consumption in urban areas than to increase production within Zambia through the ZFSP in its present form. Input subsidies could still be justified if the apparent inefficiencies were outweighed by equity considerations or a long-term sustainable development of the input sector. However, such effects are doubtful.*

As can be seen, while looking at efficiency, the study also naturally considers several other criteria including some dimensions of sustainability (e.g. what exit strategy is employed) and the impact/effectiveness of the subsidies, as well as overall impact.

Source: Baltzer and Hansen (2011[15]), *Agricultural input subsidies in Sub-Saharan Africa: Evaluation Study*, http://www.oecd.org/derec/49231998.pdf

---

Box 4.11. Evaluating efficiency at the policy level: Dutch development aid policy for improved water management

This review focused on the development aid policy for improved integrated water resource management of the Dutch Ministry of Foreign Affairs from 2006 to 2016. This was an increasingly important policy priority for the Netherlands and covered a range of partnerships with multilateral organisations, country governments, NGOs and the private sector. The two main criteria used in the evaluation were policy effectiveness and policy efficiency.

Evaluation of efficiency

The specific evaluation question used related to efficiency was formulated as follows:

- Was policy implementation adequately organised and operationalised to support achievement of the intended key results, with regard to water user groups, technical quality and maintenance of physical infrastructure?

In addressing this question, the evaluators considered the extent to which achieving key results deviated (in terms of the costs and deadlines) from what was planned and why. They considered results at each level of the results chain, including quality, outcomes and sustainability. The evaluation identified, for example, that participatory irrigation management planning was sometimes subject to delays and cost overruns as the social and technical complexity of the local issues compounded political and institutional factors, contributing to slow performance and cost overruns.

Source: IOB (2017[16]), *Tackling major water challenges: Policy review of Dutch development aid policy for improved water management*, https://english.iob-evaluatie.nl/publications/policy-review/2017/12/01/418-%E2%80%93-iob-%E2%80%93-policy-review-of-dutch-development-aid-policy-for-improved-water-management-2006-2016-%E2%80%93-tackling-major-water-challenges

Impact

Definition of impact:

Impact: What difference does the intervention make?

The extent to which the intervention has generated or is expected to generate significant positive or negative, intended or unintended, higher-level effects.

Note: Impact addresses the ultimate significance and potentially transformative effects of the intervention. It seeks to identify the social, environmental and economic effects of the intervention that are longer term or broader in scope than those already captured under the effectiveness criterion. Beyond the immediate results, this criterion seeks to capture the indirect, secondary and potential consequences of the intervention. It does so by examining the holistic and enduring changes in systems or norms, and potential effects on people's wellbeing, human rights, gender equality, and the environment.

What is impact and why is it important?

The impact criterion encourages consideration of the big "so what?" question. This is where the ultimate development effects of an intervention are considered – where evaluators look at whether or not the intervention created change that really matters to people. It is an opportunity to take a broader perspective and a holistic view. Indeed, it is easy to get absorbed in the day-to-day aspects of a particular intervention and simply follow the frame of reference of those who are working on it. The impact criterion challenges evaluators to go beyond and to see what changes have been achieved and for whom. The importance of this is highlighted in the Swedish International Development Cooperation Agency's (Sida) Evaluation Manual (Molund and Schill, 2004[17]):

> *"The impact criterion provides an important corrective to what could otherwise become an overly narrow preoccupation with the intentions of those who plan and manage development interventions and a corresponding neglect of the perspectives of target groups and other primary stakeholders."*

Although the use of the word impact is commonplace, it is important to note that there is often confusion in how it is understood, which could affect how stakeholders understand the evaluation. First, in a political context it can be used loosely to mean "results" in the broadest sense, encompassing both effectiveness and impact as defined here, as well as other aspects of performance. Second, in recent years it has often been confused with the term "impact evaluation", referring to specific methodologies for establishing statistically significant causal relationships between the intervention and observed effects.[5] When used in this way, impact may refer to results anywhere along the results chain, including outputs, and almost always refers to *desired* effects. For these reasons, it is important to clarify with stakeholders how they understand the term at the outset and explain how it is being used in the evaluation context as a criterion to examine higher-level effects.

Questions that the impact criterion might cover include:

- Has the intervention caused a significant change in the lives of the intended beneficiaries?
- How did the intervention cause higher-level effects (such as changes in norms or systems)?
- Did all the intended target groups, including the most disadvantaged and vulnerable, benefit equally from the intervention?

- Is the intervention transformative – does it create enduring changes in norms – including gender norms – and systems, whether intended or not?
- Is the intervention leading to other changes, including "scalable" or "replicable" results?
- How will the intervention contribute to changing society for the better?

Understanding impact: Elements for analysis

The definition of impact includes the key concepts of higher-level effects, significance, differential impacts, unintended effects and transformational change.

Significance

The impact criterion captures the "so what?" question of an evaluation. It examines the significance of the intervention and its higher-level results, meaning how much it mattered to those involved.

The definition is intended to encourage evaluators to consider different perspectives, according to the setting. The evaluator should think carefully about the context, as well as the needs and priorities of the intended beneficiaries of the intervention, the agreed policy goals of the relevant institutions and the nature of the intervention itself. This element for analysis can also be applied when considering an intervention's unintended results.

In assessing "significance"[6], evaluators should be aware of the importance of considering different perspectives and using a systematic approach informed by the needs of stakeholders. They should also take measures to keep their (implicit) biases and value judgements from affecting their evaluation of the intervention's significance.

Differential impact

In keeping with the SDG remit to "leave no one behind" and to safeguard human rights, including gender equality, assessing the differential impacts is important. Positive impacts overall can hide significant negative distributional effects. It is essential to consider this at the evaluation design stage, or indeed at the intervention design stage, to ensure that impact by target group can be monitored and then evaluated. This requires early planning in design and evaluation to ensure that disaggregated data is available where feasible and may also involve looking at a range of parameters around exclusion/inclusion. It will involve a granular analysis of disaggregated data where available.

Unintended effects

Evaluators should consider if an intervention has unintended effects. This analysis should include the extent to which impacts were intended or envisaged when the intervention was designed. Unintended effects can be positive or negative. Where they are positive, evaluators should consider their overall significance and whether there is scope for innovation or scaling or replication of the positive impact on other interventions. Evaluators should pay particular attention to negative impacts, particularly those that are likely to be significant including – but not limited to – environmental impacts or unintended impacts on vulnerable groups.

Transformational change

The definition defines transformational change as "holistic and enduring changes in systems or norms". Transformational change can be thought of as addressing root causes, or systemic drivers of poverty, inequalities, exclusion and environmental damage, and is recognised in the 2030 Agenda as necessary to achieving the sustainable development goals. It is becoming more and more common for interventions to aim at contributing to transformational change and evaluators are increasingly called upon to answer questions about effects on norms and systems (social, economic, or political systems), when assessing the impact criterion. For example, an evaluation might examine the extent to which traditional gender roles have been modified in some way (see Box 4.12).

Connections with other criteria

As with the other criteria, the impact criterion interacts conceptually with other criteria:

- Impact and effectiveness: Impact and effectiveness both consider what results are achieved by the intervention, effects on beneficiaries and unintended results. The difference between the two criteria will largely depend on how the intervention and its objectives were designed. Effectiveness will generally focus on the achievement of stated objectives (at any level of the results chain); impact will always focus on higher-level effects that would not otherwise automatically be considered (because they were not included as objectives). Another way to think about the distinction between the two is that over time many interventions may be rated as effective, but still not "add up" to the desired higher-level or transformational change. If impact is not evaluated, these trends will be missed. Articulations of the intended results of an intervention will vary with different institutions often having different requirements for defining the results chain. In some institutions, every intervention is required to link to higher-level goals, while in others only immediate effects are considered. In applying the two criteria, it will be useful for institutions to ensure requirements for intervention design are clear and coherent. Where smaller interventions, such as projects, do not routinely articulate how they link to higher-level goals, it is important for the evaluation policy to mandate analysis of impact – otherwise higher-level impacts will be missed (see Box 4.12 for an example).

- Impact and coherence: The fact that impact involves taking a holistic perspective means that it naturally fits well with considerations of coherence, as the effects achieved by an intervention almost always depend on other interventions, policy goals, trade-offs and the systems in which the intervention takes place. One example would be development co-operation programmes that support strengthening public health systems in developing countries, where the impact is affected not only by the programme, but also by domestic or global policies on pricing and regulation for pharmaceuticals or recruitment of health workers.

- Impact and efficiency: As noted under the efficiency criterion, in order to look at efficiency in the broadest sense, evaluators need to consider a holistic picture of the results achieved (e.g. impact, sustainability) and compare results with the resources.

- Impact and sustainability: Impact and sustainability both consider, to some extent, whether results will endure over time. Impact focuses on the time dimension in terms of examining transformational changes (which are enduring by nature). Sustainability looks at the continuation of benefits. As a criterion, sustainability is broader because it considers the conditions for achieving sustainability and the links between an intervention's economic, social and environmental sustainability.

Integrating inclusion

Transformational change, differential impact and significance are all intrinsically linked with inclusion. It is important here to understand what impact has occurred and for whom. Have there been meaningful contributions to transforming systems of oppression and could this lead to lasting change for marginalised and vulnerable groups? Evaluators should aim to understand the extent to which these unintended impacts stem from structural inequality within wider systems and the impact of interventions on these systems.

The revised definition of impact emphasises the high-level results of an intervention, including the long-term social and economic impacts. It encompasses transformative change to systems and norms including, as noted in the definition, "potential effects on people's wellbeing, human rights, gender equality and the environment". Impact is where evaluators can see the bigger picture of how an intervention contributes and adds to transformational change, equity, human rights and empowerment.

Challenges of evaluating impact and how to address them

Of all the six criteria, impact is the one that can often be the most challenging to evaluate and understand. Four of the main challenges involved, together with some suggestions on how to proceed, are summarised below.

As a guiding rule, evaluating impact typically requires more resources and considerably more primary data than for the other criteria, and should only be built into an evaluation design when these resources are likely to be available or can be obtained for this purpose. On the other hand, because it focuses on if and how the intervention has made a difference, this is the area that will often receive the most attention from users. Accordingly, the investment in time and effort to include it in the evaluation is often justifiable.

An additional challenge when evaluating impact is related to the deadlines set by the institutions that commission evaluations. These deadlines are often the same as the closing date of the intervention. This requirement could be more flexible to allow impact to be examined over a longer period of time enabling better understanding of those impacts which may only become evident after an intervention has finished.

The table below identifies several of the key challenges when evaluating impact and suggests ways of addressing them for both evaluators and evaluation managers.

Table 4.5. Challenges of evaluating impact

Challenge	How to address: Evaluators	How to address: Evaluation managers
Clarity on what impact means as a concept for the relevant stakeholders and users of the evaluation	Agree at the outset which definition is being used, whether the OECD DAC terminology or a different concept, and follow this consistently. Check with stakeholders regularly during discussions if their interpretation of the term has changed.	
Clarity on what impact was intended for this intervention and how it would be achieved	This depends on the original design of the intervention and availability of a clear results framework, with a theory of change. If this does not exist, a theory-based evaluation of impact (which is highly desirable) would be difficult, so it will need to be reconstructed which includes reference to specific target groups. Some interventions typically have goals that are too broad and inflated beyond the scope of what the intervention can achieve.	
Identifying the degree to which the intervention causes the impact	Mapping the pathways of contribution or attribution as appropriate from the intervention to results when these may be less traceable/explicit at higher levels. Use of methods such as contribution analysis can be helpful here.[7] Drawing on specific guidance/methodologies on how to measure impact, explore options and make deliberate and realistic choices on methods driven by the purpose of the evaluation, context, questions to be answered, data availability and resources available for the evaluation and their feasibility. A key question is whether the methods will simply assess the size of the impact for that intervention, or also identify why and how it occurred.	Check that the resources available for the evaluation and the skills of those involved (concerning application of methods) are sufficient to assess impact.
Availability of data including baselines and indicators	For assessing higher-level effects, data can be particularly challenging, including lack of baselines and indicators. This is partly an evaluability question to be considered at the	Establish the availability of data during the process of drafting the terms of reference for the evaluation.

	outset of the evaluation but also informs the choice of suitable methods to draw on different types of qualitative and quantitative data in the best possible way.	
The intervention has significant unexpected or unintended effects	It is often difficult to capture unintended or unexpected results as they are often left out of monitoring frameworks and data collection. To capture what is most important for beneficiaries and other people affected by the intervention (positively or negatively) evaluators should remain open to looking beyond the formal project documents and expected data. The relative significance of the effects will likely vary across stakeholders.	Provide space for the evaluators to listen to people affected by the intervention (positively or negatively) and support them in drawing attention to unexpected effects that matter to them.

Examples of evaluating impact

This section includes a cross section of examples demonstrating how impact has been evaluated for interventions related to family empowerment, peacebuilding, research support, land use planning, and violence against women and girls.

Box 4.12. Evaluating the effectiveness and impact of Colombia's "More Families in Action" programme

An evaluation of the operational and wellbeing impacts of the "More families in action" programme in Colombia provides an interesting example of how to understand and identify higher-level transformational change, including how certain aspects are evaluated under effectiveness and impact, from slightly different angles. This evaluation looked at the role of *Madres Lideres*, women trained to help implement the programme and who serve as community advocates.

- Operationally: The evaluation looked at the role of *Madres Lideres* in supporting programme effectiveness, highlighting women's critical role in implementation and delivery.

- Higher level: In addition, the evaluation identified that their involvement in the programme led to positive empowerment effects for the individual women, as well as potentially transformative effects for the broader communities by changing perceptions of women's roles in society. These higher-level changes in norms are captured under the impact criterion.

Source: Economía Urbana and Ipsos (2019[18]), *Evaluación de operaciones del programa "más familias en acción" y de resultados del componente de bienestar comunitário [Evaluation of the "More Families in Action" programme]*, https://colaboracion.dnp.gov.co/CDT/Sinergia/Documentos/Evaluacion_MFA_Informe_Resultados.pdf

---

Box 4.13. Evaluating the impact of Sida's support for peacebuilding in conflict and post-conflict affected countries

This evaluation is an interesting example of considering the impact criterion for a complex intervention over a long time period in fragile situations. Impact was assessed in terms of the overall effect of Sida's peacebuilding efforts in terms of direct, indirect, intended and unintended, positive and negative results.

This evaluation captured longer term impacts by taking a very long-term perspective, covering peacebuilding work in Somalia, Rwanda, Bosnia and Guatemala from the early 1990s until the late 2010s. In addition to overall impact it focused particularly on women and the impact on marginalised groups. The evaluation used the "most significant change" methodology to assess the contributions of the intervention.

Source: Bryld (2019[19]), *Evaluation of Sida's Support to Peacebuilding in Conflict and Post-Conflict Contexts: Somalia Country Report*, https://publikationer.sida.se/contentassets/1396a7eb4f934e6b88e491e665cf57c1/eva2019_5_62214en.pdf

Box 4.14. Evaluation of impact in a strategic policy evaluation

In an evaluation of support and research carried out by 21 Danish authorities, engaged in 40 projects in 18 partner countries, a key finding under the impact criterion was the significance of higher-level empowerment effects among partner institutions. It concluded that one of the key achievements of the intervention was to empower partner authorities beyond the formal objectives of the project. This refers to Denmark's ability to interact and connect with key public, private, civil society and development actors, and to influence the shaping of broader policy and programme outcomes. Such achievements are mutually beneficial for both partners, but mostly "fly under the radar" of intervention monitoring. However, it is an essential outcome of the programme to appreciate its full value-added.

Source: PEM Consult (2020[20]), *Evaluation of the Danish Strategic Sector Cooperation*, https://um.dk/en/danida-en/results/eval/eval_reports/publicationdisplaypage/?publicationID=CBE77158-1D4D-46E3-A81F-9B918218FAFF

Box 4.15. Evaluating impact, diffusion and scaling-up of a comprehensive land-use planning approach in the Philippines

In looking at the impact of a land-use intervention, this evaluation considered the medium- to long-term effects of the intervention, based on environmental and socio-economic indicators.

It used a theory-based approach and a mixed-methods design, drawing on panel data from a multi-level survey, qualitative interviews, focus group discussions, a literature review, a document analysis of land-use planning documents, and geographic data and information. The evaluators undertook a comprehensive reconstruction of the intervention's theory of change.

The core of this evaluation is a rigorous impact assessment that measured and quantified effects in five impact fields, ranging from improvements in administrative structures and conditions in planning administrations; the handling of natural resources; measures and activities in Disaster Risk Management; functioning of local governance, to welfare improvements for the affected population.

The panel data comprise 3 000 households, spread across 300 barangays in 100 municipalities, across 11 provinces in the Visayas region, measured at two points of time (2012 and 2016). It included households that had received assistance from the German development agency, GIZ (*Deutsche Gesellschaft für Internationale Zusammenarbeit*), and households not having received assistance. The impact assessment method also included a quasi-experimental design based around propensity score matching to identify "statistical twins", based on several dozen characteristics of the municipalities, barangays, and households.

Source: Leppert et al. (2018[21]), *Impact, Diffusion and Scaling-Up of a Comprehensive Land-Use Planning Approach in the Philippines: From Development Cooperation to National Policies*, https://www.deval.org/files/content/Dateien/Evaluierung/Berichte/2018/Zusammenfassung_Deutsch_%20DEval-2018_Philippinen_final_web-2.pdf

Box 4.16. Evaluating the impact of the "Girl Empower" programme in Liberia

This evaluation by the International Rescue Committee provides a specific example of assessing the impact of a multifaceted intervention that addresses violence against women and girls: the Girl Empower "Mentoring and Cash Transfer Intervention to Promote Adolescent Wellbeing in Liberia". This intervention was implemented in Limba county in 2016. It is a useful example of how the specific results evaluated under both effectiveness and impact will vary depending on how the goals of the intervention have been defined.

Evaluation of impact

The purpose of the study is specifically to assess the impact of one particular type of intervention aimed at addressing violence against women and girls in Liberia, i.e. adding a cash transfer component to a combined economic strengthening and gender transformative intervention for very young adolescent girls.

The evaluation collected detailed baseline and endline information on the extent of violence against young women and girls and specific effects of the intervention, both during the intervention and after one year. Outcomes were measured using a cluster-randomised, controlled trial at the village level. The research design aimed to test 1) the overall impact of the programme, compared to a counterfactual (the control) group; and 2) the effectiveness of adding a participation incentive payment ("GE+ programme"), specifically to measure if giving cash incentives to girls has protective and empowering benefits, which reduces risk of sexual violence, possibly mediated through increasing the girls' attendance of programme sessions.

Empowerment effects and changes in social norms and attitudes around girls' place in society, and about violence, would be examples of transformational impacts.

Source: Hallman et al. (2018[22]), *Girl Empower Impact Evaluation: Mentoring and Cash Transfer Intervention to Promote Adolescent Wellbeing in Liberia*, https://www.rescue.org/sites/default/files/document/4346/girlempowerimpactevaluation-finalreport.pdf

Definition of sustainability:

Sustainability: Will the benefits last?

The extent to which the net benefits of the intervention continue or are likely to continue.

Note: Includes an examination of the financial, economic, social, environmental and institutional capacities of the systems needed to sustain net benefits over time. Involves analyses of resilience, risks and potential trade-offs. Depending on the timing of the evaluation, this may involve analysing the actual flow of net benefits or estimating the likelihood of net benefits continuing over the medium and long term.

What is sustainability and why is it important?

Assessing sustainability allows evaluators to determine if an intervention's benefits will last financially, economically, socially and environmentally. While the underlying concept of continuing benefits remains, the criterion is both more concise and broader in scope than the earlier definition of this criterion.[8] Sustainability encompasses several elements for analysis – financial, economic, social and environmental – and attention should be paid to the interaction between them.

Confusion can arise between sustainability in the sense of the continuation of results, and environmental sustainability or the use of resources for future generations. While environmental sustainability is a concern (and may be examined under several criteria, including relevance, coherence, impact and sustainability), the primary meaning of the criteria is not about environmental sustainability as such; when describing sustainability, evaluators should be clear on how they are interpreting the criterion.

Sustainability should be considered at each point of the results chain and the project cycle of an intervention. Evaluators should also reflect on sustainability in relation to resilience and adaptation in dynamic and complex environments. This includes the sustainability of inputs (financial or otherwise) after the end of the intervention and the sustainability of impacts in the broader context of the intervention. For example, an evaluation could assess whether an intervention considered partner capacities and built ownership at the beginning of the implementation period as well as whether there was willingness and capacity to sustain financing at the end of the intervention. In general, evaluators can examine the conditions for sustainability that were or were not created in the design of the intervention and by the intervention activities and whether there was adaptation where required.

Evaluators should not look at sustainability only from the perspective of donors and external funding flows. Commissioners should also consider evaluating sustainability before an intervention starts, or while funding or activities are ongoing. When assessing sustainability, evaluators should: 1) take account of net benefits, which means the overall value of the intervention's continued benefits, including any ongoing costs, and 2) analyse any potential trade-offs and the resilience of capacities/systems underlying the continuation of benefits. There may be a trade-off, for example, between the fiscal sustainability of the benefits and political sustainability (maintaining political support).

Evaluating sustainability provides valuable insight into the continuation or likely continuation of an intervention's net benefits in the medium to longer term, which has been shown in various meta-analyses to be very challenging in practice. For example in sectors such as water and sanitation, or intervention types such as community driven development, benefits often fade out after some time. The role of evaluation here can be to scrutinise assumptions in the theory of change for how sustainability is achieved (Mansuri and Rao, 2013[23]; White, Menon and Waddington, 2018[24]).

If these various aspects of sustainability are carefully considered by an evaluation, it can lead to important insights into how interventions can plan and implement for change that ensures sustainable development in the future. The lessons may highlight potential scalability of the sustainability measures of the intervention within the current context or the potential replicability in other contexts.

A key aspect of sustainability is exit planning. Evaluations should assess whether an appropriate exit strategy has been developed and applied, which would ensure the continuation of positive effects including, but not limited to, financial and capacity considerations. If the evaluation is taking place *ex post*, the evaluator can also examine whether the planned exit strategy was properly implemented to ensure the continuation of positive effects as intended, whilst allowing for changes in contextual conditions as in the examples below.

A useful resource for further understanding sustainability and addressing common challenges is a meta-evaluation (Noltze, Euler and Verspohl, 2018[25]) and evaluation synthesis (Noltze, Euler and Verspohl, 2018[26]) recently conducted by the German Institute for Development Evaluation (Deval). The two studies highlight the various elements for analysis of sustainability that can be examined in an evaluation. The meta-evaluation makes a strong case for the evaluation of sustainability that incorporates the principles of the SDGs, highlighting the areas in which this can add value to an evaluation. This includes an analysis of how identifying and assessing the unintended effects of a project and the interactions or trade-offs between the different dimensions of sustainability can support learning and accountability when applying the sustainability criterion.

Understanding sustainability: Elements for analysis

To understand the definition of sustainability involves understanding the components of the enabling environment, the continuation of positive effects, and risks and trade-offs.

Building an enabling environment for sustainable development

Evaluations can consider how an intervention contributed to improving the enabling environment for development in multiple ways, including how the intervention ensured the strengthening of systems, institutions or capacities to support future development or humanitarian activity. This encourages evaluations to consider the development partner capacity that has been built or strengthened as a result of the intervention, as well as the resilience built to absorb external changes and shocks. This will ensure that the net benefits, as discussed earlier, continue into the future.

To provide examples of how the enabling environment for development can be improved, contributions of an intervention could include: capacities strengthened (at the individual, community, or institutional level); improved ownership or political will; increased national (and where applicable subnational) financial or budgetary commitments; policy or strategy change; legislative reform; institutional reforms; governance reforms; increased accountability for public expenditures; or improved processes for public consultation in development planning.

Continuation of positive effects: Actual and prospective sustainability

Sustainability can be evaluated over different timeframes. Evaluators can assess for both actual sustainability (i.e. the continuation of net benefits created by the intervention that are already evident) and prospective sustainability (i.e. the net benefits for key stakeholders that are likely to continue into the future). Evaluators should carefully consider appropriate evaluation approaches to assess actual and/or prospective sustainability, depending on the timing of the evaluation and the timescale of intended benefits. Many higher-level changes will take many years or decades to be fully realised.

In terms of evaluating actual sustainability, the evaluator can examine the extent to which any positive effects generated by the intervention demonstrably continued for key stakeholders, including intended beneficiaries, after the intervention has ended. Evaluators can also examine if and how opportunities to support the continuation of positive effects from the intervention have been identified, anticipated and planned for, as well as any barriers that may have hindered the continuation of positive effects. This can support findings that demonstrate adaptive capacity in an intervention where it was required.

Examining prospective sustainability entails a slightly different approach. An evaluation examining the future potential for sustainability would assess how likely it is that any planned or current positive effects of the intervention will continue, usually assuming that current conditions hold. The evaluation will need to assess the stability and relative permanence of any positive effects realised, and conditions for their continuation, such as institutional sustainability, economic and financial sustainability, environmental sustainability, political sustainability, social sustainability and cultural sustainability.

Risks and potential trade-offs

Assessing sustainability involves looking not only at the likelihood of continued positive effects but also an examination of the potential risks and ongoing costs associated with an intervention. Therefore, evaluation managers should consider the factors that may enhance the sustainability of net benefits over time as well as factors that may inhibit sustainability. Examining the risks related to the sustainability of an intervention can involve assessing the extent to which there are identifiable or foreseeable positive or negative contextual factors that may influence the durability of the intervention's results.

This also raises the issue of trade-offs, an important element of the revised criteria. Assessing the trade-offs associated with an intervention encourages examination of the trade-off between instant impact and potential longer-term effects or costs as well as the trade-offs between financial, economic, social and environmental aspects. For instance, an evaluation may find that an intervention supported economic growth but that this growth is unsustainable due to its major environmental costs that may negatively impact longer-term economic growth. This is in line with the SDG definition of sustainable development and broadens the scope for evaluations to examine sustainability beyond just the likelihood of continued positive effects from an intervention.

Connections with other criteria

Sustainability is closely linked with the other criteria.

- Sustainability is linked to relevance, with the level of relevance to key stakeholders being a key factor affecting their ownership and buy-in to eventual benefits, which in turn drive sustainability.
- Likewise, coherence can provide useful insights on sustainability, as it looks at other interventions in a given context, which could support, or undermine, the intervention's benefits over time.
- Effectiveness and impact: The evaluation of the continuation of results relies firstly on results having been achieved (effectiveness) and secondly, that higher-level effects were demonstrated (impact). Therefore, effectiveness and impact can be seen as overriding criteria for sustainability because if their analysis does not show the intervention achieving outputs, outcomes or impacts, there will be no clear benefits to sustain. Box 4.19 provides an example of how impact and sustainability can be examined together. Considering synergies between impact, effectiveness and sustainability by evaluating conditions that are sufficient and necessary for results to continue after the intervention has finished enables evaluators to explore effectiveness and impact over the longer term.

- Efficiency concerns may also undermine sustainability of benefits, for example when short-term costs drive decision making to the detriment of longer term effects, sustainability may be lessened.

Integrating inclusion

The revised definition of sustainability and its note draw attention to the "financial, economic, environmental and social" dimensions of sustainability and how these support the ongoing and long-term benefits of the intervention's results. Evaluators should consider how the continuation of benefits for different groups of beneficiaries has been planned for and, if the evaluation is taking place *ex post,* how this is manifest for these different groups. Here, there should be a focus on the "leave no one behind" principle and how marginalised groups experience ongoing positive benefits as well as trade-offs that may occur between different groups.

It is also relevant for evaluators to consider the extent to which the intervention has built an enabling environment for inclusive and equitable development, addressing underlying systemic issues ("treating the illness, not just symptoms") under both the impact and sustainability criteria. Questions of ownership and gender empowerment are important here. Sustainability of systems requires increased capacity so evaluators should understand whose capacity has been built and how this relates to existing unequal systems and structures. Is there both capacity and commitment from different stakeholder groups to create and uphold an enabling environment for gender equality and women's empowerment over the medium to long term? If not, what are the barriers, and are these within the scope of the intervention?

Challenges of evaluating sustainability and how to address them

The table below identifies challenges when evaluating sustainability related to timing, the lack of positive effects and other factors affecting sustainability, and suggests ways of addressing them for both evaluators and evaluation managers.

Table 4.6. Challenges of evaluating sustainability

Challenge	How to address: Evaluators	How to address: Evaluation managers
If the intervention has not achieved its intended results (assessed via effectiveness), positive unintended benefits or made contributions to impact	In the case that the intervention has had no benefits, the analysis of sustainability becomes redundant. Evaluators should be clear and open about the limitations of evaluating sustainability and consider focusing on other criteria.	Managers should consider adjusting the scope of the evaluation and redirecting resources to other criteria, including understanding why benefits were not achieved.
Timing of the evaluation	Evaluations will often take place during the lifespan of the intervention or may occur at a point where sustainability is not yet evident. Therefore, evaluators should consider focusing on the conditions for sustainability if the intervention is still being implemented or has very recently ended. They should provide a robust assessment of prospective sustainability by identifying factors in the operating environment that could favour sustainability. In this sense, gender analysis is a key and will provide useful and relevant information on the consistency of the structural changes achieved and their effect on reducing inequalities.	If the evaluation is taking place while the intervention is still active, managers should be clear on the extent to which they prioritise sustainability considerations and the purpose of examining this. For example, will findings feed into exit or transition planning?
Evaluating factors likely to influence sustainability	Contextual factors that support (or undermine) prospective sustainability can be assessed qualitatively and quantitatively. These include but are not limited to stakeholder ownership and engagement, absorptive capacity, political will and national resource availability.	Managers can help identify the relevant stakeholders to be interviewed or surveyed.

Examples of evaluating sustainability

This section gives examples from rural development in Afghanistan, general budget support and maternal health, to demonstrate how sustainability has been evaluated.

Box 4.17. Examining sustainability in an ex-post evaluation of Japan's "Inter-Communal Rural Development Project" in Afghanistan

The Inter-Communal Rural Development project was implemented as part of the Japan International Co-operation Agency's (JICA) Ogata Initiative and aimed to establish a model for community-led rural development that contributed to reconstruction and rural development outcomes in the provinces of Balkh, Bamyan and Kandahar of Afghanistan. This ex-post evaluation considered sustainability in relation to the reconstruction efforts following the civil war in Afghanistan.

Having established that the intervention had been successfully implemented and had met its objectives, the evaluation subsequently examined the sustainability of the benefits. In assessing sustainability, the evaluation analysed whether the policy, institutional, technical and financial conditions were in place to ensure continuation of positive effects. This included the capacity and willingness of the Afghan government to continue implementation after the end of the project.

The evaluation found that the intervention had established monitoring systems in co-operation with other donors, as well as a fiscal foundation utilising donors' funds, complementing and building capacity in the national system of the conflict-affected country. It was also confirmed that the Afghan government was determined to continue community-led rural development through the clustering of Community Development Councils with the support of donors. The project was also incorporated into the National Solidarity Programme. Therefore, the evaluation concluded that the policy, institutional, technical and financial conditions to ensure continued positive effects were in place and that there were no apparent risks.

Source: Watanabe (2016[27]), *Ex-Post Evaluation of Technical Co-operation Project "Inter-Communal Rural Development Project"*, https://www2.jica.go.jp/en/evaluation/pdf/2015_0603847_4.pdf

---

Box 4.18. Lessons on sustainability from the evaluation of the withdrawal of general budget support in Malawi, Rwanda, Uganda and Zambia

An interesting example of using the sustainability criterion thoughtfully in an evaluation, this study considered the extent to which the intervention adequately prepared for the continuation of positive effects after budget support ended and whether it supported the creation of an enabling environment for development. This study took place in the wake of widespread withdrawal of general budget support, starting from around 2010, due to a series of scandals in the recipient countries and accountability pressure in donor countries. This development had followed the shift in favour of budget support in the early 2000s, in reaction to the 2005 Paris Declaration on Aid Effectiveness. Budget support was widely viewed as an effective and sustainable means of supporting development results. A number of evaluations and synthesis studies provided evidence that budget support had positively affected important development outcomes such as increases in pro-poor spending, increased school enrolment and improvements in public financial management.

The evaluation utilised a comparative case study design in Malawi, Rwanda, Uganda and Zambia to evaluate whether suitable strategies had been implemented to ensure the continuation of the positive effects associated with general budget support following its withdrawal. It highlighted that, although the total level of aid remained constant in most countries in the wake of the decision to withdraw general budget support, the established structures largely disappeared. The majority of positive achievements were negatively affected or even reversed. Stand-alone project-type funding was found to be the new prevailing modality in bilateral aid portfolios with joint funding limited to a few sectors and programmes. This had led to negative externalities and high fragmentation of aid, which made it difficult to create national ownership or address systematic and broader governance issues.

Source: Orth, Birsan and Gotz (2018[28]), *The Future of Integrated Policy-Based Development Cooperation: Lessons from the Exit from General Budget Support in Malawi, Rwanda, Uganda and Zambia*, http://www.deval.org/files/content/Dateien/Evaluierung/Berichte/2018/DEval_EN_The%20Future%20of%20Integrated%20Policy-Based%20Development%20Cooperation..pdf

Box 4.19. Evaluating the impact and sustainability of DFID's maternal health programme

This review conducted by the Independent Committee on Aid Impact (ICAI) of the United Kingdom's Department for International Development's (DFID) results in improving maternal health in different countries provides an example of how impact and sustainability can be considered side by side. ICAI's reviews follow a specific approach, which in this case prioritises three main areas, namely impact, equity and sustainability. The review questions include:

- Impact: How well has DFID maximised the impact of its programming on maternal health? How robust are its claims regarding maternal health results at global, country and programme levels? How well do its investments reflect global evidence on what works in improving maternal health, and to what extent have its programmes delivered the outcomes required to improve maternal health?

- Equity: How well did the programmes target hard-to-reach and marginalised women? How well is DFID contributing to strengthening health systems and improving women's access to them?

- Sustainability: Are DFID's maternal health results likely to prove sustainable? How well has DFID supported the development and implementation of national policies and institutions to ensure sustainable results?

Equity here includes direct consideration of specific effects for poor and young women, in line with the nature of the intervention. Such questions regarding differential results and specific populations can be covered from different angles under the new definitions of relevance, effectiveness and impact. Sustainability is considered in terms of "how likely" the results are to be sustained, given that actual sustainability (*ex post*) could only be observed over a longer time period (in the future).

The methodology in this case involves making an independent assessment (in line with ICAI's role and mandate) of DFID's claims regarding the results of its work on improving maternal health, including its modelling work. It draws on documents, interviews and field visits.

Source: ICAI (2018[29]), *Assessing DFID's results in improving Maternal Health: An impact review*, https://icai.independent.gov.uk/wp-content/uploads/ICAI-review-Assessing-DFIDs-results-in-improving-Maternal-Health-.pdf

References

Arghiros, D. et al. (2017), *Making it Count: Lessons from Australian Electoral Assistance 2006-16*, Australian Government Department of Foreign Affairs and Trade, http://www.oecd.org/derec/australia/australia-electoral-assistance-2006-2016.pdf (accessed on 11 January 2021).   [11]

Baltzer, K. and H. Hansen (2011), *Agricultural Input Subsidies in Sub-Saharan Africa: Evaluation Study*, DANIDA, International Development Cooperation, Ministry of Foreign Affairs of Denmark,, http://www.oecd.org/derec/49231998.pdf (accessed on 11 January 2021).   [15]

Befani, B. and J. Mayne (2014), "Process Tracing and Contribution Analysis: A Combined Approach to Generative Causal Inference for Impact Evaluation", *IDS Bulletin*, Vol. 45/6, pp. 17-36, http://dx.doi.org/10.1111/1759-5436.12110.   [31]

Belcher, B. and M. Palenberg (2018), "Outcomes and Impacts of Development Interventions", *American Journal of Evaluation*, Vol. 39/4, pp. 478-495, http://dx.doi.org/10.1177/1098214018765698.   [34]

Bryld, E. (2019), *Evaluation of Sida's Support to Peacebuilding in Conflict and Post-Conflict Contexts: Somalia Country Report*, Sida, https://publikationer.sida.se/contentassets/1396a7eb4f934e6b88e491e665cf57c1/eva2019_5_62214en.pdf (accessed on 11 January 2021).   [19]

Chambers, R. et al. (2009), "Designing impact evaluations: different perspectives", No. 4, 3ie, https://www.3ieimpact.org/evidence-hub/publications/working-papers/designing-impact-evaluations-different-perspectives (accessed on 11 January 2021).   [35]

Economía Urbana and IPSOS (2019), *Evaluación de operaciones del programa "más familias en acción" y de resultados del componente de bienestar comunitario*, [Evaluation of the "More Families in Action" programme], Departamento Nacional de Planeación, Bogotá D.C., https://colaboracion.dnp.gov.co/CDT/Sinergia/Documentos/Evaluacion_MFA_Informe_Resultados.pdf (accessed on 15 January 2021).   [18]

Eurecna Spa (2020), *Bolivia - Evaluation of Health Initiatives (2009-2020)*, Italian Ministry of Foreign Affairs and International Cooperation, http://www.oecd.org/derec/italy/evaluation-report-of-health-initiatives-in-Bolivia-2009_2020.pdf (accessed on 11 January 2021).   [5]

FAO (2020), *Evaluation of "Improving farmer livelihoods in the dry zone through improved livestock health, productivity and marketing"*, Food and Agriculture Organization of the United Nations, Rome, http://www.fao.org/3/ca8463en/ca8463en.pdf (accessed on 11 January 2021).   [4]

Gertler, P. et al. (2016), *Impact Evaluation in Practice: Second Edition*, World Bank Group, Washington D.C., https://publications.iadb.org/en/impact-evaluation-practice-second-edition (accessed on 12 January 2021).   [30]

Global Affairs Canada (2019), *Evaluation of Natural Disaster Reconstruction Assistance in the Philippines, 2013-14 to 2018-19*, Global Affairs Canada, https://www.international.gc.ca/gac-amc/publications/evaluation/2019/endra-earcn-philippines.aspx?lang=eng (accessed on 12 January 2021).   [8]

Hallman, K. et al. (2018), *Girl Empower Impact Evaluation: Mentoring and Cash Transfer Intervention to Promote Adolescent Wellbeing in Liberia*, International Rescue Committee, https://www.rescue.org/sites/default/files/document/4346/girlempowerimpactevaluation-finalreport.pdf (accessed on 12 January 2021). [22]

ICAI (2018), *Assessing DFID's Results in Improving Maternal Health: An Impact Review*, The Independent Commission for Aid Impact, https://icai.independent.gov.uk/wp-content/uploads/ICAI-review-Assessing-DFIDs-results-in-improving-Maternal-Health-.pdf (accessed on 11 January 2021). [29]

IDD and Associates (2006), *A Joint Evaluation of General Budget Support Evaluation of General Budget Support: Synthesis Report*, https://www.oecd.org/development/evaluation/dcdndep/37426676.pdf (accessed on 11 January 2021). [2]

IDEV (2018), *Cabo Verde: Evaluation of the Bank's Country Strategy and Program 2008–2017: Summary Report*, Independent Development Evaluation, African Development Bank, http://www.oecd.org/derec/afdb/AfDB-2008-2017-cabo-verde-bank-strategy.pdf (accessed on 11 January 2021). [12]

IEG (2008), *The Welfare Impact of Rural Electrification: A Reassessment of the Costs and Benefits*, World Bank, http://dx.doi.org/10.1596/978-0-8213-7367-5. [14]

IOB (2017), *Tackling major water challenges: Policy review of Dutch development aid policy for improved water management*, Policy and Operations Evaluation Department, Ministry of Foreign Affairs, Netherlands, https://english.iob-evaluatie.nl/publications/policy-review/2017/12/01/418-%E2%80%93-iob-%E2%80%93-policy-review-of-dutch-development-aid-policy-for-improved-water-management-2006-2016-%E2%80%93-tackling-major-water-challenges (accessed on 12 January 2021). [16]

Leeuw, F. and J. Vaessen (2009), *Impact Evaluations and Development: NoNIE Guidance on Impact Evaluation*, The Networks on Impact Evaluation, Washington D.C., http://search.oecd.org/dac/evaluation/dcdndep/47466906.pdf (accessed on 12 January 2021). [33]

Leppert, G. et al. (2018), *Impact, Diffusion and Scaling-Up of a Comprehensive Land-Use Planning Approach in the Philippines: From Development Cooperation to National Policies*, German Institute for Development Evaluation (DEval), Bonn, https://www.deval.org/files/content/Dateien/Evaluierung/Berichte/2018/Zusammenfassung_Deutsch_%20DEval-2018_Philippinen_final_web-2.pdf (accessed on 12 January 2021). [21]

Mansuri, G. and V. Rao (2013), *Localizing Development*, The World Bank, http://dx.doi.org/10.1596/978-0-8213-8256-1. [23]

Ministry of Foreign Affairs Japan (2019), *Japan ODA Evaluation Guidelines*, https://www.mofa.go.jp/policy/oda/evaluation/basic_documents/pdfs/guidelines11th.pdf (accessed on 18 February 2021). [6]

Molund, S. and G. Schill (2004), *Looking Back, Moving Forward Sida Evaluation Manual*, Sida, https://www.oecd.org/derec/sweden/35141712.pdf (accessed on 11 January 2021). [17]

Noltze, M., M. Euler and I. Verspohl (2018), *Evaluation Synthesis of Sustainability in German Development Cooperation*, German Institute for Development Evaluation (DEval), Bonn, http://www.deval.org/files/content/Dateien/Evaluierung/Berichte/2018/DEval_Evaluierungssyn these_EN_web.pdf (accessed on 12 January 2021). [26]

Noltze, M., M. Euler and I. Verspohl (2018), *Meta-Evaluation of Sustainability in German Development Cooperation*, German Institute for Development Evaluation (DEval), Bonn, http://www.deval.org/files/content/Dateien/Evaluierung/Berichte/2018/DEval_NH_Meta-Evaluierung_EN_web.pdf (accessed on 12 January 2021). [25]

Norad (2018), *Evaluation of Norwegian Efforts to Ensure Policy Coherence for Development*, Norad, https://www.norad.no/contentassets/4ac3de36fbdd4229811a423f4b00acf7/8.18-evaluation-of-norwegian-efforts-to-ensure-policy-coherence-for-development.pdf (accessed on 11 January 2021). [7]

OECD (2011), *Evaluating Budget Support: Methodological Approach*, DAC Network on Development Evaluation, OECD Publishing, Paris, https://www.oecd.org/dac/evaluation/dcdndep/Methodological%20approach%20BS%20evalu ations%20Sept%202012%20_with%20cover%20Thi.pdf (accessed on 12 January 2021). [3]

OECD (2010), *Quality Standards for Development Evaluation*, DAC Guidelines and Reference Series, OECD Publishing, Paris, https://dx.doi.org/10.1787/9789264083905-en. [1]

OECD (2002), *Evaluation and Aid Effectiveness No. 6 - Glossary of Key Terms in Evaluation and Results Based Management (in English, French and Spanish)*, OECD Publishing, Paris, https://dx.doi.org/10.1787/9789264034921-en-fr. [10]

Orth, M., M. Birsan and G. Gotz (2018), *The Future of Integrated Policy-Based Development Cooperation: Lessons from the Exit from General Budget Support in Malawi, Rwanda, Uganda and Zambia*, German Institute for Development Evaluation (DEval) , Bonn, http://www.deval.org/files/content/Dateien/Evaluierung/Berichte/2018/DEval_EN_The%20Fut ure%20of%20Integrated%20Policy-Based%20Development%20Cooperation..pdf (accessed on 12 January 2021). [28]

Palenberg, M. (2011), *BMZ: Tools and Methods for Evaluating the Efficiency of Development Interventions | Managing for Sustainable Development Impact*, BMZ Evaluation Division – German Federal Ministry for Economic Cooperation and Development, http://www.managingforimpact.org/resource/bmz-tools-and-methods-evaluating-efficiency-development-interventions (accessed on 12 January 2021). [13]

PEM Consult (2020), *Evaluation of the Danish Strategic Sector Cooperation*, Evaluation, Learning and Quality Department, Ministry of Foreign Affairs/Danida, Denmark, https://um.dk/en/danida-en/results/eval/eval_reports/publicationdisplaypage/?publicationID=CBE77158-1D4D-46E3-A81F-9B918218FAFF (accessed on 12 January 2021). [20]

Slovenia's Ministry of Foreign Affairs (2017), *Evaluation of Slovenia's Development Cooperation with Montenegro 2013-2016: Final Report*, Slovenia's Development Cooperation, https://www.gov.si/assets/ministrstva/MZZ/Dokumenti/multilaterala/razvojno-sodelovanje/Development-cooperation-with-Montenegro-evaluation-final-report.pdf (accessed on 12 January 2021). [9]

UNEG (2013), *Impact Evaluation in UN Agency Evaluation Systems: Guidance on Selection, Planning and Management*, http://www.uneval.org/document/detail/1433 (accessed on 12 January 2021). [32]

Watanabe, K. (2016), *Ex-Post Evaluation of Technical Cooperation Project "Inter-Communal Rural Development Project"*, JICA, https://www2.jica.go.jp/en/evaluation/pdf/2015_0603847_4.pdf (accessed on 12 January 2021). [27]

White, H., R. Menon and H. Waddington (2018), "Community-driven development: does it build social cohesion or infrastructure? A mixed-method evidence synthesis", No. 30, 3ie, https://www.3ieimpact.org/evidence-hub/publications/working-papers/community-driven-development-does-it-build-social-cohesion (accessed on 12 January 2021). [24]

Notes

[1] The term "beneficiaries" is defined as, "the individuals, groups, or organisations, whether targeted or not, that benefit directly or indirectly, from the development intervention". Other terms, such as "rights holders" or "affected people" may also be used.

[2] There may be instances where two institutions participate in an intervention, one as the implementing partner and another one as the funder. It is possible in this configuration to assess internal coherence from the perspectives of both the funder and the implementing partner.

[3] An important caveat to this is that evaluating impact is much more likely to be useful when it is accompanied by an analysis of how impact is achieved and what can be done to increase impact versus when it is purely an accountability exercise.

[4] A detailed and comprehensive discussion on methodological options for defining and assessing efficiency is set out in a BMZ working paper by Palenberg (2011[24]) which identifies three different levels: Level 0: Describing and providing an opinion on some efficiency-related aspects of an aid intervention. Level 1: Identifying efficiency improvement potential within an aid intervention. This provides a partial picture of the implementation processes, costs of inputs, conversion of inputs into outputs or conversion of outputs into outcomes. Level 2: Assessing the efficiency of an aid intervention in a way that it can be compared with alternatives or benchmarks. This is a comprehensive approach that includes a reliable estimate of all major benefits and costs.

In practice, level two assessment is rarely applied. Even an organisation with huge capacity such as the World Bank had noted by 2010 that there had been a large decline in application of cost-benefit analysis at the appraisal stage, even in the sectors where it was most applicable. The report highlighted the positive aspects in terms of rigour and links to subsequent project performance of using such a depth of analysis, but also the challenges involved (IEG, 2010[25]). The example of rural electrification (IEG, 2008[26]) is a relatively rare example of a full level two analysis. Other options available to evaluators include multi-criteria decision making/modelling. It is also important to note that such types of efficiency analysis are more likely to be applicable in certain sectors, for example, infrastructure, health and agriculture. An interesting example from agriculture on input subsidies, which uses a country case study approach drawing on a range of economic estimates and survey data, is cited in Box 4.10.

[5] The literature on this topic is abundant but see for example: UNEG (2013[32]); Chambers et al (2009[35]); Leeuw and Vaessen (2009[33]); Belcher and Palenberg (2018[34]), and Gertler et al (2016[30])

[6] Not to be confused with statistical significance, which often comes up under certain types of impact evaluations; see Gertler et al. (2016[30]) which discusses power calculations and related technical concepts in quantitative impact evaluations.

[7] See Befani and Mayne (2014[31]).

[8] The *2002 Glossary* (OECD, 2002[10]) definition of sustainability is: "The continuation of benefits from a development intervention after major development assistance has been completed. The probability of continued long-term benefits. The resilience to risk of the net benefit flows over time."

.

www.ingramcontent.com/pod-product-compliance
Lightning Source LLC
Chambersburg PA
CBHW082111210326
41599CB00033B/6663